Anger Management for Men

A Complete Guide To Taking Control Of Your Anger, Mastering Your Emotions, And Building A Balanced Life

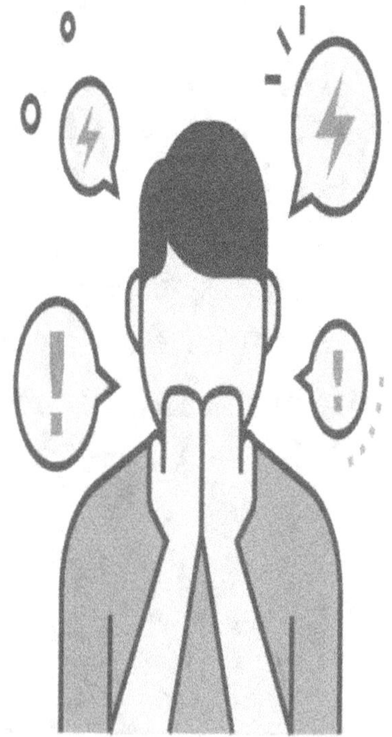

Copyright Page

Table Of Content

Introduction:
Confronting the Silent Storm

Anger is a powerful emotion that wells up intensely, often suddenly, and has a significant impact on the lives of those it touches. In many ways, anger is a silent storm that, if not understood or effectively managed, can have devastating effects on mental and physical health, relationships, and personal growth. This introduction is intended to illuminate the nuances of anger as it pertains to men specifically, and to provide insight into its complex nature, its specific impact on men, and the purpose of this guide to help individuals manage, control, and ultimately transform anger into a positive power.

• Overview of Anger's Complex Role

Discuss anger as a powerful, often misunderstood emotion that can both drive and derail personal well-being.

Anger is an emotion deeply rooted in human nature, woven into our evolutionary history as a survival mechanism. It can be a powerful motivator, a catalyst, propelling us into action when we experience injustice, feel threatened, or feel our boundaries are being crossed. Although anger is constructive and empowering, giving us the courage to speak out against injustice or stand up for ourselves, it is often misunderstood and stigmatized as an inherently destructive force.

In essence, anger is neither good nor bad. She is

just there. The key is to understand those dualities. When expressed constructively, anger promotes self-esteem, resilience, and positive change. But when anger is uncontrolled or misdirected, it can affect personal well-being and lead to cycles of hostility, isolation, and regret. Uncontrolled anger often makes decision-making difficult, strains relationships, and undermines mental and emotional balance.

The complexity of anger stems from its deep connection to other emotions. Under the surface, anger can hide feelings of weakness, sadness, fear, and disappointment. However the intensity of anger can mask these underlying emotions, and men often end up reacting reactively rather than reflexively. This e-book attempts to unravel the layers of anger by exploring its origins, triggers, and the profound impact it has on a person's thoughts, actions, and interactions.

- ## Men and Anger

Explain why anger is particularly impactful in men's lives due to social conditioning, stressors, and internal expectations.

For many men, anger occupies a unique and powerful place on the emotional spectrum heavily influenced by societal expectations, stressors, and internalized ideals of masculinity. From an early age, men are often raised to perceive emotions such as sadness, fear, and even joy as weaknesses, with anger being one of the few "acceptable" emotional expressions. This conditioning can lead to an over-reliance on anger as a coping mechanism -- an outlet for other repressed emotions that don't have room for expression.

The pressures of modern life further reinforce this reliance on anger. Men face stressors related to work demands, family responsibilities, economic pressures, and societal expectations to be resilient providers and protectors. This relentless pressure creates a cycle in which anger becomes a default response and a shield against perceived weakness. This shapes not only men's relationships with others, but also with themselves, as unresolved anger can distort self-image, decrease self-compassion, and stunt emotional growth.

Furthermore, men's anger can be exacerbated by a lack of resources or opportunities for healthy expression. Traditional norms can prevent men from seeking support or openly exploring their feelings, allowing their anger to fester without a constructive outlet. This sense of isolation can increase feelings of frustration and make anger more difficult to control. Understanding and considering these unique factors is essential to developing effective anger management strategies tailored to men's life experiences and emotional environments.

• Purpose of this guide

Purpose of the Guide: Outline how this book aims to provide practical, sustainable strategies to harness and manage anger constructively.

The purpose of this book, "Anger Management for Men: A Complete Guide to Controlling Anger, Mastering Emotions, and Building a Balanced Life," is to provide practical, sustainable strategies to help men constructively control and deal with anger. This guide recognizes that anger if understood and effectively channeled, can be a source of power and a driver of personal growth.

This book aims to go beyond addressing the symptoms of anger to explore the underlying causes and patterns that fuel it. Readers are led on a journey of self-discovery to explore the roots of anger, the situations that trigger it, and the unique impact anger has on their lives. This guide aims to give men the tools to recognize and manage their anger before it escalates, turning moments of anger into opportunities for insight and change.

In addition to immediate techniques to control anger, the guide also offers long-term strategies to increase emotional intelligence, build resilience, and cultivate mindfulness. By focusing on self-awareness and emotion control, the book helps men change their approach to anger from reactive to reflective, promoting healthier, more fulfilling relationships and stronger self-awareness.

Ultimately, this e-book aims to give men the opportunity to take control of their emotional world. Through a combination of psychological insights, practical exercises, and relatable examples, *Anger Management for Men* offers a guide to balance, leading readers to a more peaceful and self-determined way of life.

Chapter 1

Understanding Anger's Roots

- *What is Anger?*

Explore anger as a multifaceted emotional response, including its physiological, psychological, and behavioral dimensions.

Anger is a powerful and often complex emotion that results from a dynamic interplay of physiological, psychological, and behavioral factors. Depending on the person, the situation, and the underlying triggers, it can occur as a sudden wave of irritation or escalate into intense rage. Although anger is pervasive in everyday life, it remains one of the most misunderstood emotions, with both constructive and destructive potential. To better manage anger, it is important to explore the multifaceted nature of anger and understand how it manifests in the body, mind, and behavior.

Physiological Aspects of Anger

Anger is deeply rooted in our physiological responses. It is a primitive, automatic response designed to protect us from threats, and has evolved over millennia as part of the body's "fight or flight" response. When we perceive a threat, be it physical, emotional, or social, our body activates a complex cascade of responses to prepare for self-defense or decisive action. These responses are controlled by the autonomic nervous system, particularly the sympathetic nervous system, which releases hormones such as adrenaline and cortisol.

When Anger Is Triggered, Several Physiological Changes Occur:

- **Increased heart rate and blood pressure:** Anger increases your heart rate, causing your body to pump more blood in preparation for possible action. Your blood pressure increases, and you often feel a flush in the face or a sense of heat.

- **Muscle tension:** Muscles, especially in the face, neck, and hands, tense up and prepare for movement, so you may feel stiff and want to clench your fists or jaw. Improved breathing and energy levels: Breathing becomes shallower and faster, providing more oxygen to the body and supporting the fight-or-flight response. Blood sugar levels may also increase, increasing energy stores.

- **Cognitive focus on threat:** Anger narrows your focus on the perceived danger or source of frustration, reducing your ability to fully process information. This tunnel vision is part of an adaptive response to dealing with an immediate threat.

These physiological changes occur rapidly, sometimes within seconds, and can be overwhelming or difficult to control. For those who suffer from chronic anger, these repeated physical stress responses can take a toll on the body and lead to long-term health problems, such as cardiovascular disease, suppressed immune system, and increased risk of anxiety and depression.

Psychological Aspects Of Anger:

Psychologically, anger is not just a reflexive reaction. It is a complex emotional experience that is shaped by our thoughts, perceptions, past experiences, and personality traits. Anger often arises in response to feelings such as injustice, frustration, fear, and helplessness. How we interpret an event or situation plays a key role in the intensity of our anger. For example, two people may react very differently to the same situation depending on how they interpret it. One may feel insulted or disrespected, while the other may dismiss it as a minor issue.

- **Cognitive triggers:** Anger is often triggered by certain thoughts or beliefs. These may include "should" statements (e.g., "You should respect me"), assumptions about other people's intentions, or a focus on past grievances. This internal dialogue can reinforce feelings of injustice or hurt, increasing anger.

- **Personal values and expectations:** Anger is often tied to a person's values and personal boundaries. When these values and boundaries are challenged, anger may emerge as a defensive reaction, demanding recognition or support of these values.

- **Personality factors:** Some personality traits, such as impulsivity, hostility, and perfectionism, may cause certain people to experience anger more frequently or more intensely. People who see the world as competitive or hostile may also be more easily provoked.

- **Masking emotions:** Anger may act as a mask for more vulnerable emotions such as sadness, fear, and shame. When people feel that these emotions are unacceptable or difficult to express, anger becomes a secondary emotion, masking these emotions and giving a sense of control or power.

The psychological aspects of anger can be difficult to manage because they involve deeply ingrained thought patterns and emotional responses. Cognitive-behavioral techniques that reframe thoughts and challenge beliefs can be very effective tools to address the psychological components underlying anger.

Behavioral Aspects Of Anger.

Behavioral, anger can manifest itself in a variety of behaviors, from subtle expressions of irritation to overtly aggressive behavior. When anger reaches a critical point, there is often an instinctive need to act to signal displeasure or right an injustice. This behavior can take many forms, including verbal statements, physical actions, and passive-aggressive behavior.

- **Expressive behavior:** The most direct behavioral response to anger is verbal expression, such as yelling, harsh words, and sarcasm. Expressing anger verbally can provide temporary relief, but if left uncontrolled, it can damage relationships and lead to unfortunate situations.

- **Aggressive behavior:** In some cases, anger can manifest as physical aggression, ranging from slamming doors to physical altercations. Aggression is the most visible and destructive expression of anger and it has long-term effects on both the individual and those involved.

- **Suppression and passive-aggression:** Not all anger is openly displayed. Some people suppress their anger, which can lead to passive-aggressive behavior. This may include silence, veiled comments, or self-destructive behavior. Suppressed anger may seem less harmful on the surface, but it can create resentment and a negative emotional atmosphere.

- **Constructive responses:** When anger is channeled correctly, it can encourage constructive behaviors, such as B. Setting boundaries and defending yourself or working toward a solution. Healthy expression of anger is assertive without being aggressive and respectful of both yourself and others.

Understanding these behavioral responses to anger is crucial because behavior is often what others react to and judge. Furthermore, behaviors become habitual, and over time those who suffer from chronic anger may develop unhealthy patterns of behavior that make it difficult for them to respond constructively.

The Interconnected Nature of Anger's Dimensions

The physiological, psychological, and behavioral aspects of anger do not operate in isolation. They are closely related and influence each other in feedback loops. For example, a physiological response such as a sudden increase in heart rate may intensify the psychological experience of anger by increasing the arousal of the emotion, which in turn may lead to more intense behavioral expression.

Similarly, a cognitive belief, such as feeling disrespected, may also trigger both physical and behavioral responses. Recognizing this interconnectedness can help individuals recognize how these dimensions interact and ultimately cause anger to feel overwhelming or uncontrollable. By understanding the separate yet interconnected nature of the various aspects of anger, people can approach anger more holistically and learn to implement strategies that address their whole experience, not just one aspect of anger.

Conclusion:

Towards a balanced understanding of anger. Anger is a complex emotional response that requires careful understanding and management. Although anger is often portrayed negatively, it plays an important role in life, from protection to inspiring action. When effectively channeled, anger can promote self-esteem, strengthen relationships, and inspire change. However, when ignored or mishandled, it can be destructive, undermining health, relationships, and self-image. The way to manage anger is to embrace its complexity and recognize its physiological, psychological, and behavioral levels. This understanding forms the basis of the tools and strategies featured in this guide, enabling readers to transform silent storm anger into a force for growth, resilience, and balance.

• Common Triggers and Underlying Causes of Anger

Examine root causes, such as unresolved pain, stress, and unmet needs that commonly ignite anger.

Anger is rarely an isolated reaction to a specific event. It often reflects deeper feelings, unmet needs, or past experiences that reinforce our reaction. Examining the common triggers and root causes of anger can provide insight into why certain situations evoke this strong emotion. Understanding these roots - unresolved pain, chronic stress, unmet expectations, and deep-rooted patterns - can be transformative, allowing you to address and manage anger before it escalates. Recognizing these factors is key to transforming anger from a reactive emotion into a constructive force.

1. Unresolved Pain and Hurt

Anger is often a by-product of unresolved pain or past wounds. Experiences such as betrayal, loss, rejection, and abuse can leave lasting scars and resurface as anger, especially when similar situations or past memories occur. For example, someone who experienced neglect in childhood may be more sensitive to rejection and feel intense anger when rejected or ignored as an adult. This is not a reaction to the present moment alone, but a cumulative reaction that comes with unhealed pain.

- **Past Trauma Triggers:** People with unresolved trauma may react angrily to situations that others perceive as minor. For example, someone who has experienced betrayal may react strongly to perceived infidelity or dishonesty, even if the current situation does not call for such a strong reaction.

- **Protecting You From Vulnerability:** Because pain is unresolved, we often build walls to protect ourselves from being hurt again. Anger acts as a defense mechanism to push others away or to control situations that make us feel unsafe. This anger-based defense can strain relationships and hinder personal growth because it keeps us from working on healing and moving on from past pain.

Understanding that unresolved pain is a trigger for anger allows us to self-reflect with compassion. Recognizing these issues opens the door to healing and can significantly reduce the frequency and intensity of angry reactions.

2. Chronic Stress And Pressure In Daily Life

Stress is a major cause of anger, especially in today's fast-paced, stressful world. When faced with ongoing demands such as financial difficulties, work pressures, family responsibilities, and health problems, stress can reach a breaking point. Anger is often an outlet for pent-up tension, even if the triggering event seems trivial.

- **Everyday hassles as a stress limiter:** Stress can magnify reactions to everyday irritations like traffic delays, minor disagreements, and household chores. For people who experience chronic stress, these small annoyances can trigger tantrums because they add an extra hurdle to an already stressful day.

- **Stress and impatience:** Chronic stress can cause irritability and a shortened tolerance threshold, which can result in a "blowout fuse." People under stress are more likely to react quickly and violently to irritations, and anger is the primary outlet for this pent-up energy.

- **Physical effects of stress on anger:** Stress triggers the body's "fight or flight" response, increasing heart rate, blood pressure, and cortisol levels. This heightened physical state can make anger feel more intense and harder to control because the body is primed for action. Prolonged stress can make people more agitated, angry, and unable to control their emotions.

Learning to recognize and manage stress through practices such as mindfulness, relaxation, and setting healthy boundaries can help reduce angry reactions. Addressing the root of stress can prevent it from building up and leading to anger.

3. Unmet Needs and Unfulfilled Expectations

People have a range of emotional, physical, and psychological needs, from safety and belonging to respect and recognition. When these needs are not met, anger can arise as a sign that something is missing or out of balance. Anger often reflects disappointment or frustration due to unmet expectations, or feelings that one's needs are being ignored or unrecognized.

- **Need for respect and recognition:** Many people feel anger when they feel they are not respected or valued. This is especially true in situations where one feels their efforts are ignored or undervalued, such as in work or relationships. The need for recognition is a basic human need, and when it is not met, anger can become a way of asserting one's own worth or limitations.

- **Expectations in relationships:** Expectations play a key role in anger, especially in intimate relationships. Anger can flare up when we expect support, honesty, and empathy from our partners, friends, and family, and those expectations are not met. This may be done to communicate the depth of our disappointment or to emphasize the importance of an unmet need.

- **Personal values and integrity:** Anger can also result from situations in which personal values are violated or ignored. For example, someone who values honesty may become upset when they perceive deception, even if the deception is minor. This reaction is not only related to the situation itself but also to a perceived threat to one's core beliefs and integrity.

Identifying unmet needs and setting realistic expectations can reduce the intensity of anger when those needs are not met. Practicing assertive communication and self-reflection can help people express their needs constructively, rather than letting anger dictate their reactions.

4. Learned Patterns And Social Conditioning

Anger is also influenced by learned behaviors and

social conditioning. Men, in particular, are often taught to express strength and resilience rather than vulnerability and sadness. As a result, anger can become the default expression for a range of emotions, from sadness to fear. These learned patterns can make anger seem like the most familiar or socially acceptable way to process difficult emotions.

- **Cultural Expectations:** Society often conditions men to be stoic and self-sufficient, leaving little room for emotional expression. Anger is seen as a symbol of strength, whereas weakness may be perceived as weakness. Over time, this conditioning can result in anger becoming the default response to situations that seem threatening or overwhelming.

- **Family background and role models:** Home environment also plays a key role in how people express anger. People who grew up in homes where anger was either expressed explosively or completely suppressed are likely to reflect these patterns in adulthood. If they don't learn healthy ways to process and express their emotions, they may repeat destructive anger cycles or struggle to regulate their emotions.

- **Peer influence and social identity**: Peers can heighten angry responses, especially during their formative years. People may view anger as a means of control or status and may behave in an angry way to fit in, gain approval, or demonstrate superiority. These influences can form deep-rooted patterns that are difficult to break.

Recognizing the role of learned behavior and social conditioning can help individuals question and reframe their responses to anger. Relearning emotional expression through healthier ways of expressing yourself can help replace destructive patterns with constructive behaviors.

5. Insecurity and Low Self-Esteem

Deeper emotions of insecurity and low self-esteem are frequently concealed by anger. When a person doubts their self-worth or feels inadequate, anger serves as a protective mechanism to fend off those feelings. This is especially true in situations that trigger feelings of shame or embarrassment, where anger can become a tool to avoid weakness.

- **Fear of being judged:** People with low self-esteem may react angrily when criticized or blamed. This anger becomes a shield that protects them from feelings of inadequacy and failure. For example, a person may lash out at someone who questions their decisions or abilities. The reason is that hidden in the anger is a deep fear of "not being good enough."

- **Sensitivity to rejection:** Uncertainty often leads to increased sensitivity to rejection or perceived disrespect. When a person feels unaccepted or excluded, anger comes to the forefront to combat the feelings of inferiority that the situation provokes. This can lead to defensive anger that is disproportionate to the actual situation.

Building self-esteem and emotional resilience is a key step in managing anger that stems from anxiety. Addressing the sources of self-doubt can help you face criticism or rejection with confidence and reduce the urge to react with anger.

Conclusion:

Turning insight into action

Understanding the common triggers and underlying causes of anger can provide a guide to dealing with this powerful emotion more constructively. Recognizing that anger often stems from unresolved pain, chronic stress, unmet needs, learned behaviors, and anxiety can help you address these issues head-on and transform anger from a reactionary force into an opportunity for growth. By practicing self-reflection, increasing emotional awareness, and developing healthy ways of expressing your needs and feelings, you can build a healthier relationship with your anger and use it as a signal rather than letting it dictate your behavior.

• Impact of Unchecked Anger on Life

Detail the toll of unregulated anger on mental health, relationships, career, and physical well-being

Uncontrolled anger has far-reaching effects that go far beyond the moment of anger or frustration. When anger becomes chronic, intense, or uncontrollable, it can lead to destructive patterns that affect many areas of life, including mental health, relationships, professional success, and even physical health. Anger is a natural emotion, but when left uncontrolled, it can lead to harmful behaviors and emotional instability that affect not only the person feeling the anger but also those around them. Understanding the harmful effects of uncontrolled anger highlights the urgency and importance of developing effective anger management skills.

1. Impact On Mental Health

Uncontrolled anger has serious effects on mental health, often leading to emotional exhaustion, anxiety, and depression. When anger persists, the mind goes into an agitated state, preventing one from attaining calm and emotional stability. Over time, this constant mental arousal can erode a person's emotional resilience and make them more vulnerable to other mental health problems.

- **Chronic stress and anxiety:** Anger keeps the brain in a state of hyperarousal similar to the "fight or flight" response. This constant activation of the nervous system increases cortisol levels, which puts a strain on the body's stress response and causes chronic anxiety. People who experience frequent anger may feel constantly on edge and unable to relax or find inner peace.

- **Depression and Guilt:** People who suffer from uncontrollable anger often feel guilty or remorseful after an angry outburst. This cycle (anger followed by guilt) can lead to feelings of worthlessness and self-criticism, which over time can lead to depression. This cycle erodes self-esteem and leads to feelings of helplessness and hopelessness.

- **Impaired Emotion Regulation:** Chronic anger can weaken your ability to effectively regulate your emotions. Over time, this lack of emotional regulation creates an unstable internal state, where any trigger, no matter how small, can trigger an intense emotional reaction, leading the sufferer to feel that they have little control over their mental state. This disrupted regulation has a negative impact on overall well-being, as it promotes a chaotic and unstable mental situation.

Investing in anger management strategies is essential to maintaining mental health. By learning how to communicate and express anger in constructive ways, people can protect their mental health and promote a more balanced emotional life.

2. Strained Relationships And Social Isolation

Uncontrolled anger can seriously damage relationships. Anger often manifests itself in negative behaviors, such as yelling, criticizing, or ignoring others, which can alienate family, friends, and colleagues. Over time, uncontrolled anger creates an atmosphere of fear and mistrust, undermining the foundations of relationships and often leading to social isolation.

- **Communication Disorders:** Anger prevents clear and open communication, resulting in misunderstandings and a lack of empathy. When anger dominates interactions, meaningful dialogue can be impeded and understanding can be replaced by defensiveness. Partners, friends, and family may feel misunderstood or attacked, which can lead to distance and emotional barriers.

- **Loss of trust and intimacy:** In romantic relationships, uncontrolled anger can erode trust and intimacy. When one partner frequently reacts with anger, the other may withdraw, feel insecure or unappreciated. This withdrawal damages intimacy and creates an emotional gap that is difficult to fill, leaving both partners feeling isolated and bitter.

- **Impact on parenting and family relationships**: Uncontrolled anger can also affect parenting, setting up a vicious cycle of anger in children as their own emotional response. Parents who struggle with anger may often yell or express frustration at their children, creating an atmosphere of fear and resentment. Children who frequently experience anger may internalize these behaviors, which can lead to their own emotional and anger problems.

- **Social isolation:** When anger continues to affect relationships, it can lead to social isolation. Friends and family may begin to distance themselves, and the person may find it increasingly difficult to make new contacts. This isolation can increase feelings of loneliness and make it more difficult to gain support and perspective, ultimately worsening their mental and emotional state.

Dealing with anger issues in relationships requires honest communication, empathy, and sometimes professional counseling. By recognizing how anger affects those close to you, you can take meaningful steps to improve your relationships and build stronger, more supportive connections.

3. Career Setbacks And Professional Impacts

- Uncontrolled anger can negatively impact your career and damage relationships with colleagues, superiors, and customers. In a professional environment, the ability to control emotions and communicate respectfully is crucial. Uncontrolled anger can lead to impulsive decisions, strained work relationships, and damaged reputations.

- **Damaged Professional Relationships:** Anger expressed in the workplace can lead to conflicts, misunderstandings, and the breakdown of professional relationships. Colleagues may avoid or begin to distrust angry people, isolating them and undermining team cohesion. Trust and respect are essential in a professional environment, but uncontrolled anger can quickly undermine both.

- **Decreased Work Performance and Productivity:** Anger clouds judgment and affects concentration, making it difficult for individuals to perform at their best. Mental energy expended to maintain or suppress anger comes at the expense of the energy needed to complete tasks, solve problems, and make informed decisions. This can lead to reduced productivity, missed deadlines, and mistakes, ultimately jeopardizing professional success.

- **Reputation and career advancement:** Uncontrolled anger can damage an individual's reputation within an organization or industry. Those known for having a "short fuse" may be left out of promotions or important projects because their superiors question their ability to handle stress and work effectively with others. This stagnation leads to frustration and resentment, creating a cycle in which anger continues to affect career development.

- **Increased chances of losing your job:** In extreme cases, uncontrolled anger can lead to disciplinary action or even dismissal. Employers value a harmonious work environment, and people who frequently show anger may go against the company's code of conduct. Losing your job due to anger issues can lead to financial instability and a damaged professional reputation, making it difficult to find future employment.

Improving your emotional control and developing constructive ways to manage stress are essential to professional success. Managing anger effectively can help you maintain better relationships in the workplace, increase your productivity, and build a positive reputation, all of which contribute to a successful and fulfilling career.

4. Impact On Physical Health

Anger doesn't just affect your mental health and relationships. It also has significant effects on your physical health. Uncontrolled anger activates the body's stress response, releasing adrenaline and cortisol. If this continues chronically, it can lead to a variety of health problems. Over time, these physical effects can affect a person's overall health and increase the risk of serious health problems.

- **Cardiovascular Health:** Chronic anger is associated with high blood pressure, increased heart rate, and increased risk of heart disease. Repeated activation of the body's stress response puts undue stress on the cardiovascular system, raising blood pressure and increasing the likelihood of heart attack and stroke.

- **Suppresses the immune system**: Prolonged anger weakens the immune system, making you more susceptible to illness and infection. Cortisol, which is released in response to anger and stress, suppresses the effectiveness of the immune system. This means that the body's ability to fight common illnesses and maintain overall health is reduced. Digestive problems: Anger can also affect the digestive system, causing problems like stomach pain, acid reflux, and irritable bowel syndrome (IBS). The stress hormones released during anger alter the digestive process, often slowing it down or causing discomfort that can become chronic if anger is not controlled.

- **Sleep problems:** People who are chronically angry may have trouble sleeping because heightened arousal interferes with the body's ability to relax. This can lead to insomnia or difficulty sleeping, both of which affect mental and physical health, creating a vicious cycle in which lack of sleep makes frustration and anger worse.

- **Chronic pain and inflammation:** Anger is associated with increased levels of inflammation, which has been linked to a variety of chronic pain conditions such as arthritis, headaches, and muscle tension. Increased inflammatory responses in the body caused by stress and anger can exacerbate existing pain, contribute to the development of new problems, and lead to ongoing physical discomfort.

Managing anger through stress reduction techniques, physical activity, and healthy outlets can reduce these physical effects. By taking proactive steps to reduce anger, people can improve their physical health and improve their quality of life.

- **Bottom line:** Control the effects of anger Uncontrolled anger has a ripple effect, affecting every aspect of life, from mental health and relationships to professional success and physical health. Recognizing the consequences of uncontrolled anger is the first step to change. Addressing the roots of anger and developing healthy coping mechanisms can help protect your physical and mental health, maintain positive relationships, and lead a more balanced and fulfilling life. Developing your anger management skills not only enhances your personal well-being, it also helps create a more peaceful and supportive environment for all involved.

Chapter 2

The Physiology of Anger

- ### *How the Body Responds*

Explain the "fight or flight" mechanism and how anger activates adrenaline, cortisol, and other stress responses.

Anger is more than just a mental feeling. It sets off a powerful chain reaction throughout the body, triggering a physical response that prepares us to face a perceived threat. When anger arises, the body activates the "fight or flight" system, a primitive response that evolved over centuries to protect us from danger. This physiological response involves a cascade of hormones and neurotransmitters that heighten our senses, increase our physical strength, and speed up our reflexes, making it ideal for survival situations. But in modern life, where stressors are often more psychological than physical, these intense physical reactions can have long-term negative effects if left unchecked. Understanding the physiology of anger can provide valuable insight into how this emotion affects health and how to manage it.

The "Fight or Flight" Response: Priming the Body for Action

When we face a perceived threat, the body's sympathetic nervous system activates the "fight or flight" response, a complex biological mechanism that prepares us to either face or run from danger. In response to an anger-inducing situation, the brain's amygdala (the structure that processes emotions, especially those related to fear and aggression) sends a distress signal to the hypothalamus, the brain's command center for autonomic processes. This signal activates the adrenal glands, which release adrenaline and other stress hormones to prepare the body for strenuous exercise.

- **Heart rate and blood pressure:** One of the principal recognizable reactions of heart rate and blood pressure: Adrenaline entering the bloodstream causes the heart to pump faster, delivering more oxygen to muscles and giving the body energy. This increased blood flow helps a person physically protect themselves, but over time, the frequent rises in blood pressure caused by anger can put a strain on the cardiovascular system.

- Breathing and oxygen intake: When the fight-or-flight response begins, breathing becomes faster and shallower to deliver more oxygen to the muscles. This can feel like hyperventilation and often leads to dizziness and shortness of breath. Chronic anger or stress can cause long-term breathing problems as the body repeatedly enters this heightened state of readiness.

- Muscle tension: When anger arises, muscles tense up as a way of preparing the body for a possible confrontation. You may feel this tension in your neck, shoulders, jaw, and fists. Chronic anger can cause persistent muscle tension, leading to problems like headaches and muscle pain, and ultimately chronic stress conditions like tension headaches and migraines.

The Role of Anger Hormones: Adrenaline and Cortisol

The hormones released during anger not only increase your alertness but also your willingness to react. Two key hormones are central to this response: adrenaline and cortisol.

- **Adrenaline (epinephrine):** Adrenaline is released by the adrenal glands and is often referred to as the "fight or flight" hormone. It rushes through the body quickly, raising your heart rate, boosting your energy supply, and increasing focus. Adrenaline prepares the body for immediate action, whether that means landing a blow or fleeing a threat. Although effective in the short term, repeated release of adrenaline due to chronic anger can lead to sleep disorders, anxiety, and increased cardiovascular risk.

- **Cortisol:** Cortisol is known as the body's primary stress hormone, with a slightly longer-lasting role than adrenaline. Cortisol regulates several bodily functions, including blood pressure, blood sugar, and metabolism, helping to maintain a high state of alertness in the body. In situations of anger, cortisol helps prolong the body's willingness to confront the current situation. However, chronic anger, which repeatedly activates cortisol production, can impair the immune system, elevate blood sugar levels, and disrupt digestion, which can lead to long-term health problems such as high blood pressure, diabetes, and gastrointestinal disorders.

Psychological Responses Amplify Physical Reactions

The mind-body connection is particularly evident in the physiological phenomenon of anger. Psychological reactions such as increased focus decreased attention, and increased sensitivity to threats all reinforce the physical changes that anger brings about. When anger flares up, the body prioritizes functions necessary for survival and ignores non-essential systems, which can lead to digestive problems, dry mouth, and a weakened reproductive system. This prioritization is helpful in immediate survival scenarios, but problematic in everyday situations where an angry response is common but not always necessary.

Long-term effects of frequent angry responses

Although occasional anger is natural and has limited long-term health effects, frequent and uncontrolled anger can cause significant wear and tear on the body. Regular activation of the fight-or-flight response creates a chronic state of stress, which negatively impacts physical and mental health.

- **Cardiovascular health:** Constant surges of adrenaline and cortisol put a strain on the heart and blood vessels. Chronic anger is associated with an increased risk of high blood pressure, stroke, and heart disease. Research suggests that people who frequently feel and express anger are at higher risk for heart disease than those who manage their anger effectively.

- **Immune function:** When released in small amounts during acute stress, cortisol has an anti-inflammatory effect. But chronic anger and the resulting prolonged release of cortisol weaken the immune system over time, making the body more susceptible to infections and autoimmune diseases and slowing recovery from illness.

- **Mental health and cognitive function:** Chronic anger affects not only the body but also the mind. Repeated activation of the fight-or-flight response due to anger can reduce mental clarity and increase anxiety, which may contribute to depression. If cortisol levels remain elevated, memory and cognitive function may be impaired because this hormone disrupts neural pathways in the brain, especially areas associated with learning and memory, such as the hippocampus.

- **Digestive health:** Because anger ignores digestion, frequent angry reactions can lead to stomach pain, acid reflux, and other gastrointestinal problems. Chronic anger can disrupt normal digestive processes and cause symptoms such as irritable bowel syndrome (IBS) and chronic indigestion.

Practical Steps To Address Physical Reactions To Anger

To manage the physiological response to anger, you need to develop habits that calm your body and reduce stress hormones. Here are some approaches:

- **Deep Breathing:** Deep, slow breathing stimulates the parasympathetic nervous system, helping to suppress the fight-or-flight response. Breathing exercises slow down your heart rate, reduce muscle tension, decrease adrenaline production, and return your body to a state of rest.

- **Mindfulness and Meditation:** Mindfulness exercises teach people how to observe their emotional and physical states without immediately reacting. By developing a mindfulness habit, people can learn to recognize early signs of anger and use calming techniques before it escalates. Meditation can also reduce cortisol levels and improve overall stress tolerance.

- Physical Activity: Regular physical activity helps you process stress hormones like adrenaline and cortisol in a healthy way. Exercise lowers baseline stress levels, improves cardiovascular health, and elevates mood. Activities like walking, running, and yoga provide a safe outlet for physical energy while also helping to regulate the physiological effects of anger.

- **Progressive Muscle Relaxation:** Because anger often causes muscle tension, progressive muscle relaxation can help relieve this tension. By tensing and then slowly relaxing each muscle group, you can release physical tension and reduce the overall intensity of your anger. Increase your awareness of the physical signs of anger.

Building Awareness of Anger's Physical Cues

Increasing your awareness of the physical signs of anger can help people intervene in angry reactions at an earlier stage. Common early warning signs include clenching of fists, grinding of teeth, shallow breathing, and increased heart rate. Recognizing these signs can help people begin to use calming techniques before anger fully escalates. This proactive approach can prevent anger from taking over the body and mind, allowing for a more deliberate and thoughtful response to anger-provoking situations.

Understanding the physiology of anger is essential for effective anger management. By recognizing how anger affects your body, you can develop strategies to control the intensity of your anger, reduce its frequency, and mitigate its long-term health effects. This knowledge can transform anger from an overwhelming force into a controllable response, leading to improved well-being, healthier relationships, and greater resilience to life's challenges.

• Recognizing Physical Signs of Anger

Guide readers to identify physical cues like increased heart rate, clenched muscles, and tense breathing.

Anger isn't just offered as a viewpoint or feeling. It results in a series of physical changes that act as early warning signs, allowing sufferers to recognize and control their emotions before they escalate. These physical signals are often subtle at first, but as anger builds, they intensify, indicating that the body is preparing for a possible conflict. Recognizing these signals is an essential skill when dealing with anger, as doing so can allow the affected person to intervene early and prevent anger from reaching a boiling point where the reaction becomes difficult to control. Let's explore some of the most common physical signs of anger, how they manifest, and why anger is a valuable indicator of growing tensions.

1. Increased Heart Rate: The First Warning Sign

One of the most immediate physical reactions to anger is an increased heart rate. The feeling of your heart pounding or racing is part of your body's automatic "fight or flight" response, which releases adrenaline and primes your body for action. This increased heart rate is your body's way of pumping more oxygen-rich blood to your muscles, giving them the energy they need for intense physical activity.

Recognizing your elevated heart rate can be a clear signal that your anger is building. Paying attention to this signal can help you take a step back, breathe, and consciously work on calming yourself down. Techniques like deep breathing and counting can help slow your heart rate, creating space for a more considered response rather than an impulsive one.

2. Muscle Tension: The Body Braces for Action

Muscle tension is another common physical sign of anger. When someone starts to get angry, certain muscle groups tend to tense up, especially the neck, shoulders, jaw, and fists. This is because the body is preparing for a possible conflict. In intense moments, this physical stiffness serves the purpose of preparing the body for action, but in everyday situations, it can cause discomfort or even pain if left unchecked.

Noticing when muscles are tense is a valuable self-awareness tool. For example, noticing a clenched fist or clenched jaw can serve as an opportunity to stop and think about why the body is reacting the way it does. By noticing this tension, you can work on physically loosening these muscles, which can help ease feelings of anger and release pent-up frustration before they escalate.

3. Tensed and Shallow Breathing: Oxygen Flow Signals Stress

Another common response to anger is a change in breathing patterns. As anger grows, people often start to take short, shallow breaths, an automatic response aimed at quickly providing oxygen to the body. While this type of breathing is part of preparing the body for physical activity, shallow breathing can also create a feeling of tension and cause dizziness or lightheadedness. Habitually breathing shallowly in stressful situations reinforces the stress-anger cycle over time, making it difficult to remain calm.

Learning to recognize this breathing pattern when it occurs can be extremely helpful. Taking a few minutes to slow down your breathing and practice deep, even breathing can help activate your body's relaxation response. This change in breathing can reduce the intensity of your anger and increase your clarity, making it easier to calmly deal with the situation.

4. Increased Body Temperature And Sweating: Fever As A Symptom Of Anger

For many people, a noticeable increase in body temperature accompanies feelings of anger. The surge of adrenaline can make your skin turn red or feel hot, and you may start to sweat, especially on your forehead, palms, and back. This physiological response is another way the body prepares for a potential threat. Sweating cools the body and prevents overheating during moments of intense exertion.

Recognizing when your body feels unusually warm or when you begin to sweat can be a subtle but powerful cue to stop and evaluate your emotional situation. These physical sensations act as early indicators, providing an opportunity to take proactive measures such as removing yourself from the situation, practicing cooling breathing techniques, or splashing cold water on your face to reduce feelings of heat or tension.

5. Narrowed Focus And Increased Perception

Although it may not be as obvious, anger can also cause a sense of heightened focus or a narrowed field of vision, focusing on the source of your irritation, sometimes to the exclusion of everything around you. This shift in focus is part of the body's survival instinct and allows the individual to pay close attention to what they perceive as a threat. While this can be helpful in life-threatening situations, in everyday life it often leads to poor judgment and impulsive reactions.

Recognizing when you feel like you have limited focus can be a helpful step in dealing with anger. By noticing this intense focus, the individual can expand their awareness and choose to mentally step back and see the situation from a broader perspective. This awareness can help turn logic back on, balance emotional responses, and prevent anger from dictating behavior.

6. Tense and frustrated facial expressions

Physical signs of anger often appear on the face long before words are spoken. Frowning, clenching the jaw, pursing the lips, and other facial expressions are outward signs that the body is angry. While these expressions may be unconscious, noticing them in you can be an early indicator to start using calming techniques before the anger escalates further.

Recognizing these facial expressions is one way to become more aware of how anger builds up. Gently relaxing your facial muscles by taking a few deep breaths or doing facial calming exercises can be incredibly effective in reducing the intensity of your anger. This relaxation can also reduce the social impact of your visible anger, leading to improved interactions with others.

7. Stomach Pain And Discomfort

The mind and body are closely connected, and emotions are often expressed as physical sensations in the gut. For some people, anger can cause upset stomach, nausea, and indigestion. The gut is highly sensitive to emotional stress and is sometimes called the "second brain," and can reflect a person's emotional state even before they are fully conscious.

Paying attention to your intuition or noticing a sudden upset in your stomach could be a sign that anger is rising. This awareness prompts you to think about what is bothering you and helps you identify anger in its early stages. Practicing relaxation techniques or drinking a glass of water can help reduce this discomfort and reduce overall stress.

Using Body Awareness To Control Anger

Paying attention to the physical signs of anger gives you a valuable tool to manage this powerful emotion. Body signals often arrive before you even realize you are angry, providing a golden opportunity to address the emotion early and avoid reactive behavior. Here are some practical steps to deal with physical danger signals:

- **Breathing exercises:** Practicing deep diaphragmatic breathing can calm your nervous system and reduce many of the physical responses associated with anger.

- **Progressive muscle relaxation:** Tense and then relax each muscle group, helping to release physical tension, especially in areas such as the neck, shoulders, and jaw.

- **Mindfulness and body scan:** Mindfulness exercises that examine tension in the body allow individuals to identify and relax specific areas where anger may be anchored.

- **Take a short walk.** Exercise releases an adrenaline rush, allowing the body to use the energy generated by anger in a constructive way.

Recognizing and responding to these physical signals is the first step to effective anger management, allowing you to deal calmly and thoughtfully with emotionally charged situations. Practicing this bodily mindfulness helps people gradually transform anger from a destructive force into an energy that can be understood, controlled, and ultimately used in positive ways.

• Long-Term Health Effects:

Discuss the impact of chronic anger on heart health, immune function, and cognitive wellness.

Chronic anger, often unrecognized or suppressed, can silently undermine many aspects of your health, gradually damaging your body and mind. This prolonged emotional state not only increases stress but also triggers many physiological responses that impact your long-term well-being. Its effects are far-reaching, affecting vital systems such as the heart, immune system, and cognitive function. Here we examine how uncontrolled anger invades the body's basic health mechanisms and how addressing it can protect your long-term health.

1. Heart Health: The Toll of Anger on the Cardiovascular System

One of the most direct and well-documented effects of chronic anger is its impact on the cardiovascular system. Anger triggers the "fight or flight" response, causing the body to release stress hormones like adrenaline and cortisol. When anger becomes a daily stressor, this response becomes excessive, putting a near-continuous strain on the cardiovascular system. This leads to a series of effects, including:

- **Elevated Blood Pressure:** Anger causes blood vessels to constrict, increasing your heart rate and causing persistent high blood pressure. Chronic hypertension is a major risk factor for heart disease, stroke, and a variety of other cardiovascular diseases.

- **Increased risk of heart attack and stroke:** Studies have shown that episodes of intense anger can double or even triple the chance of having a heart attack or stroke immediately following the emotional episode. Prolonged stress and elevated blood pressure can increase plaque buildup in your arteries over time, which can lead to cardiovascular events.

- **Irregular heartbeat:** Chronic anger disrupts the heart's natural rhythm, contributing to arrhythmia, or irregular heartbeat. In the long term, this can damage the structure and function of the heart.

Controlling your anger is key to reducing these cardiovascular risks. Techniques like mindful breathing, regular exercise, and relaxation practices can help counteract the negative effects of anger on the heart.

2. Immune Function: The Negative Effects of Anger on the Immune System

Continuous, simmering anger has a significant impact on the immune system, primarily through the stress hormone cortisol. High cortisol levels reduce immune function over time, making the body more susceptible to infection and disease. When anger is unresolved, it essentially shifts the body's resources to a "fight or flight" response at the expense of immune defenses. This change impacts your immune system in several ways:

- **More susceptible to illness:** Prolonged anger reduces your body's ability to fight off common pathogens, making infections like colds and the flu more frequent. This weakened immune system is especially worrisome for people who have had illnesses in the past.

- **Inflammation and chronic disease:** Chronic anger is associated with increased levels of inflammation throughout the body. This persistent state of inflammation is linked to diseases like autoimmune diseases, joint pain, and even arthritis. Inflammation can also contribute to more serious diseases like diabetes and cancer, as chronic stress and anger dysregulate your immune system.

- **Slower healing and recovery:** Your immune system's ability to heal and recover from injury or illness is slowed by chronic anger. Even minor health problems may take longer to resolve because cortisol and other stress-related chemicals affect your body's ability to repair tissues and fight infections.

To protect their immune health, people who suffer from chronic anger should practice regular relaxation exercises, establish stress reduction habits, and find constructive outlets for their anger, such as through exercise or creative pursuits.

3. Cognitive Health: The Effects of Anger on Mental Clarity and Brain Health

Anger doesn't just affect the body; it also changes how the brain functions. Chronic anger can impair cognitive function, especially in areas related to decision-making, memory, and emotional control. Prolonged exposure to the stress associated with anger can have the following effects on the brain, leading to poorer cognitive function:

- **Impaired Decision-Making and Emotional Control:** Anger activates areas of the brain associated with survival instincts, such as the amygdala, while areas responsible for logical thinking, such as the prefrontal cortex, and is less active. Over time, this imbalance can affect your ability to make sound decisions, solve problems, and think clearly under stress.

- **Memory loss and decreased learning ability:** Chronic anger and stress can increase cortisol levels and damage the hippocampus, an area important for memory formation and storage. This can make it difficult to learn new information, recall memories, and focus on tasks. Over time, these problems can affect your daily life and cause cognitive decline.

- **Increased risk of neurodegenerative diseases:** Some research suggests that prolonged anger and stress may increase your risk of developing neurodegenerative diseases, such as Alzheimer's disease and other dementias. This association is due to persistent inflammation and oxidative stress caused by anger, which can damage neurons and accelerate cognitive aging.

To maintain cognitive health, it is important to adopt strategies to reduce the effects of chronic anger. Activities such as mindfulness meditation, cognitive behavioral techniques, and other mental training can help control anger and protect brain function. Participation in intellectual activities, a healthy diet, and adequate sleep also contribute to long-term cognitive health.

The path to a healthier life:

Breaking the cycle of chronic anger the long-term effects of uncontrolled anger are profound and far-reaching, affecting all major systems of the body. Recognizing the negative effects of chronic anger can be a driving force for developing better anger management skills, protecting your health, and improving your quality of life. Strategies to break the cycle of anger include:

- **Self-awareness and reflection:** By recognizing your personal anger triggers and how anger impacts your health, you can begin to make conscious changes in your behavior and mindset.

- **Build resilience through relaxation:** Regularly practicing relaxation techniques such as deep breathing, yoga, and progressive muscle relaxation can help counteract the physiological effects of anger on heart health, immune function, and cognitive health.

- **Seek support:** Working with a therapist or joining an anger management group can provide valuable support, guidance, and accountability. Therapy often provides effective tools to uncover and address unresolved emotional issues that may be contributing to chronic anger.

Learning how to deal with anger constructively not only preserves your health but also gives you a greater sense of control and satisfaction in your life. By investing in healthier anger responses, the path to long-term wellness is not only achievable but sustainable, promoting both physical and mental health.

Chapter 3:

Self-Awareness: The First Step in Anger Control

- ## Importance of Self-Awareness:

Emphasize the need for recognizing anger's signs before it become overwhelming.

Self-awareness is the foundation of effective anger management. Before productive change can occur, a person must understand and recognize their inner signs and causes of anger. In this chapter, we explore the critical role of self-awareness not only in identifying the causes of anger and emotional reactions but also in changing how we respond to and manage anger over time.

If left unchecked or misunderstood, anger can quickly become overwhelming, leading to explosive reactions or silent rage. The capacity to notice and comprehend one's own ideas, emotions, and actions is known as self-awareness. Through increased self-awareness, people gain a deeper understanding of their emotional triggers, physiological responses, and the psychological roots of their anger. This clarity allows them to pause, reflect, and choose more constructive ways to express or manage their anger.

- **Recognize the Early Warning Signs:** Anger rarely springs from nowhere. There are often subtle clues, both physical and mental, that herald their approach. These signs may include physical sensations like a racing heart, clenched fists, and shallow breathing, as well as emotional changes like irritability and restlessness. Paying attention to these early signals gives you the opportunity to address anger before it escalates. Recognizing these signs not only prevents escalation but also puts you in better control of your own emotional world.

- **Understand Triggers and Patterns:** Self-awareness involves identifying specific situations, people, or events that trigger anger. For some, these triggers may be rooted in past experiences, such as unresolved trauma or unmet emotional needs, while for others; they may arise from current stressors, such as work pressures, relationship conflicts, or societal expectations. Exploring these triggers can help people recognize patterns and understand why certain situations trigger anger. This understanding allows you to predict, avoid, or respond differently to these triggers in the future.

- **Explore the Emotional Layers of Anger:** Anger is often a secondary emotion that masks more vulnerable feelings like pain, fear, or frustration. Without self-awareness, people may not realize that they are using anger as a shield to protect themselves from these deeper uncomfortable emotions. By peeling back the layers, confident people can find the true emotions behind their anger. This insight allows them to address the core issues and respond in healthier, more constructive ways, leading to greater emotional resilience and well-being.

- **Promoting Mindfulness to Manage Anger:** Mindfulness – presence and non-judgmental awareness – promotes self-awareness by encouraging people to observe their thoughts and feelings as they arise. Regularly practicing mindfulness helps people recognize when they start to feel angry, even if they don't immediately react with anger. This creates a mental "pause" between trigger and reaction, allowing for more thoughtful and conscious action. This mindfulness practice enhances self-awareness, allowing people to deal with anger more calmly and constructively.

- **Create a Personal Anger Inventory:** Self-awareness is often enhanced through introspection and conscious observation. Keeping an anger diary or writing down the moments when anger arises can provide valuable insights. The inventory allows people to record specific triggers, immediate reactions, and physical and emotional sensations experienced. Over time, this practice can help people recognize recurring patterns, gain insight into their emotional reactions, and evaluate their progress in anger management.

- **Develop a language of emotions:** A key part of self-awareness is understanding and correctly naming emotions. Many people have difficulty distinguishing between emotions such as anger, frustration, disappointment, and resentment, and end up lumping them all together under the label "anger." Developing a more sophisticated vocabulary for emotions allows a person to better recognize what they are actually feeling and express it in a more constructive way. Instead of reacting with generalized anger, they may realize that they are actually feeling misunderstood, unsafe, or unsupported, which can lead to more effective communication and problem-solving.

- **Gain Perspective and Reduce Reactive Responses:** Self-awareness helps people take a step back and view situations more objectively. Instead of getting stuck in a reactive cycle, confident people are able to ask themselves the questions, "Why am I feeling this way?" or "What do I want to achieve with this reaction? "This ability to pause and reflect is converting. Doing so allows them to make conscious decisions that are consistent with their long-term well-being, rather than making impulsive reactions that they may later regret.

The Role of Self-Awareness in Long-Term Anger Management

Self-awareness is more than just the ability to control one's anger when it arises. It is also important for making long-term changes in emotion regulation. Working on improving self-awareness allows people to understand themselves more deeply and to better control their emotional reactions. This is the key to breaking negative patterns and building resilience.

- **Building the Foundation of Emotional Intelligence:** Self-awareness is the foundation of emotional intelligence and includes the ability to recognize, understand, and manage emotions. Increasing self-awareness allows you to better manage your emotions in a balanced way, even in stressful or difficult situations. This emotional intelligence allows you to stay calm under pressure, communicate effectively and make more rational decisions in the moment.

- **Transforming Relationships through Improved Self-Understanding:** Self-confidence doesn't just affect you as an individual. It also has an effect on relationships. When people understand their anger triggers and reactions, they are less likely to project their frustrations onto others. This leads to healthier communication, deeper connections, and more empathy in relationships. Confident people are able to approach conflicts with patience, understanding, and a desire to resolve problems constructively, rather than reacting defensively or hostilely.

- **Create lasting behavioral change:** Developing self-awareness is often the first step to creating lasting change in anger responses. As people gain insight into their feelings and reactions, they can set specific goals for changing their behavior. For example, they might choose to practice deep breathing exercises when they feel anger building up inside or take a break before reacting to a stressful situation. These targeted strategies based on self-awareness allow them to gradually steer their behavior in a more positive direction.

- **Promotes personal growth:** Embracing self-confidence is a path to personal growth and self-discovery. It invites people to face parts of themselves that they have overlooked or avoided. This journey can be difficult because it often involves uncomfortable truths, but it ultimately helps people control their anger and live a more balanced and fulfilling life. Confident people are more resilient, adaptable, and embracing change; all of which are essential qualities for a balanced, mentally healthy life.

Make self-confidence a lifelong habit

Self-confidence is not a one-time thing. It is an ongoing practice that deepens over time. As people become more aware of their anger triggers, emotions, and reactions, they are equipped with the tools necessary to effectively manage their anger. Through this commitment to self-awareness, we can transform our relationship with anger from a destructive force to a source of insight and personal growth. Understanding ourselves on a deeper level unlocks the potential to build healthier relationships, make more conscious decisions, and cultivate a greater sense of peace and well-being.

Self-awareness is the first step to controlling anger, but its benefits go beyond simply controlling anger; it is a fundamental skill for living a more conscious, self-determined, and emotionally intelligent life. When people make self-awareness a priority, it lays the foundation for lasting change, personal growth, and a more harmonious life. This chapter is an invitation to embark on this transformative journey and embrace self-awareness as an essential component of effective anger management and overall well-being.

• Identifying Personal Triggers

Help readers reflect on specific people, events, or memories that act as anger triggers.

To effectively manage anger, it is important to understand personal triggers. These triggers can be specific people, events, or memories that evoke intense emotions and impulsive reactions that can cause regret or harm. This section explains the importance of identifying personal triggers, helps readers reflect on past experiences and identify recurring patterns, and gives them the tools to navigate these situations with greater awareness and control.

The Power Of Triggers That Cause Anger

Anger rarely occurs in a vacuum. It is often triggered by external stimuli that appeal to unresolved feelings or deeply held beliefs. Identifying personal triggers is an exercise in self-discovery and emotional intelligence, giving people the insight to understand what causes their anger. If a person is aware of their triggers, they can avoid or defuse situations that may escalate their emotions. This proactive approach not only reduces impulsive outbursts but also promotes a sense of control and calm in difficult situations.

Triggers vary greatly from person to person. For some, past experiences in which they felt misunderstood or disrespected can lead to certain types of comments triggering anger. For others, anger arises in response to events that make them feel out of control or remind them of past situations. Exploring and recognizing these patterns can help people better understand how their past shapes their present reactions.

Consider Specific People As Triggers.

Certain people can be strong anger triggers, often due to the history and dynamics of the relationship. Family members, romantic partners, coworkers, and even strangers can trigger anger if interactions with them touch on unresolved issues or unhealed emotional wounds. For example, a person may feel intense anger when interacting with a family member who repeatedly invalidates their feelings or undermines their accomplishments. In this context, anger is often not just about the current interaction, but is rooted in accumulated experiences. Reflection questions to identify specific people as triggers include:

- Are there people I always feel angry or annoyed with when I interact with them?
- Do these people remind me of past situations or people that made me feel powerless or unheard?
- Are there recurring themes or specific behaviors from these people that trigger my anger?

Answering these questions honestly can help you identify recurring themes and uncover why certain people trigger anger. For example, a person might realize that they feel angry toward an overly critical boss because they remind them of a parent who was never satisfied with their performance. This awareness does not necessarily change the other person's behavior, but understanding why one reacts the way one does can allow an individual to respond differently.

Exploring Event and Situational Triggers

Certain events and situations can also trigger strong anger reactions. Traffic jams, long lines, disagreements at work, and conflicts on social media are common examples. These situations often trigger feelings of frustration, helplessness, or injustice, which trigger deeper emotional responses. Examining why certain events trigger anger can reveal an individual's values, beliefs, and unmet needs. For example:

- Traffic jams and delays can be especially triggering for people who value punctuality and control. When their day is interrupted by factors outside of their control, they can experience frustration that can quickly escalate into anger.

- Disagreements and conflicts in a professional environment can trigger feelings of inadequacy and fear of failure, especially if the person has experienced criticism or a lack of recognition in the past. In this case, the anger may stem from a deeper need to be noticed, valued, and respected.

To think about these patterns, you should ask yourself questions like:

- In what situations do you most often feel anger arise?
- Are there certain events that trigger anger sooner or more intensely than others?
- Do these situations have common elements, such as feeling disrespected, not listened to, or trapped?

Identifying situational triggers can help individuals avoid these scenarios or prepare to deal with them with a new mindset. For example, someone who recognizes that they are frustrated by being stuck in traffic can use this time to listen to calming music or their favorite podcast, turning a potential trigger into an opportunity to relax rather than tense up.

The Role Of Memories And Past Experiences In Triggering Anger

Memories can act as powerful anger triggers, especially if there are unresolved feelings from past experiences. Current interactions and situations can bring back memories of hurt, betrayal, or setbacks from long ago. These memories shape the lens through which we interpret current events, making our current reactions more intense. For instance, somebody who experienced torment in youth might feel overpowering outrage when they feel somebody disregarding them, regardless of whether the aim was not destructive.

Understanding how past experiences influence current triggers is an important part of self-awareness. Questions to reflect on include:

- Are there specific memories that come to mind when I feel angry?
- Do certain places, smells, or sounds remind you of difficult experiences from the past?
- How do these memories influence my current reactions to certain people and events?

By recognizing these memories and the emotions associated with them, a person can begin to separate the pain of the past from the current situation. This separation reduces the intensity of angry reactions and allows you to deal with current situations with greater clarity and emotional balance.

Techniques for Identifying Personal Anger.

Triggers The process of identifying personal triggers can be deeply introspective and requires patience and honesty. Here are some techniques to help people identify and understand the sources of their anger:

1. **Keep a trigger journal:** Writing down the moments when anger arises can provide valuable insight into specific triggers. This

might include writing down the people involved, the situation, thoughts, emotions, and physical sensations. This journal will eventually highlight trends and reoccurring triggers.

2. **Consciously reflect:** Taking time each day to reflect on one's own emotional experiences promotes awareness. When anger arises, a person may pause and ask themselves what triggered that emotion, what thoughts or memories surfaced, and whether a specific event or person was involved.

3. **Explore emotional patterns in therapy or coaching:** Working with a therapist or coach can help some people gain deeper insight into what triggers anger. A professional can help you recognize patterns that are difficult to detect alone, especially if they are based on long-held or unconscious beliefs.

4. **Recognize physical signals:** Anger often manifests physically before it is fully recognized mentally. Paying attention to physical signals like heartbeat, jaw clenching, and muscle tension can act as an early warning system for anger. When these signals occur, patients can take a step back and understand what triggered the physical reaction.

Respond to triggers with awareness and intention.

Once people identify their triggers, they can begin to develop strategies to respond more consciously. Instead of reacting impulsively, they can use self-awareness to manage their reactions constructively. This might mean doing deep breathing exercises, reframing their thoughts, or removing themselves from triggering situations until they feel more in control.

When a person consciously faces their triggers, they are able to take control of their emotional responses. Recognizing triggers is not about avoiding or denying anger, but rather understanding the roots of it and learning how to channel it in a way that aligns with their personal values and goals. The process of identifying and managing triggers is a journey toward emotional maturity and resilience that leads to healthier relationships, better stress management, and a more balanced life.

By knowing their anger triggers and understanding why they evoke strong emotions, people can take the first step toward managing their emotional responses. This knowledge enables them to approach their anger with curiosity and compassion, laying the foundation for long-term transformation and a deeper sense of inner peace.

• Developing Emotional Insight

Guide readers to probe deeper into what their anger reveals about themselves, including fears, insecurities, or unmet expectations.

Emotional insight is a transformational tool that allows people to go beyond immediate feelings of anger and discover what it reveals about their inner world. Anger often acts as a surface emotion - a reaction to deeper feelings such as fear, anxiety, unmet expectations, or past hurts. By developing emotional insight, readers learn to interpret what their anger is telling them about their underlying needs, values, and vulnerabilities, leading to increased self-awareness and emotional maturity.

Understanding Anger as a Messenger of Deeper Emotions

Anger can sometimes feel simple, but it is rarely a standalone emotion. Anger often arises when other feelings such as pain, fear, or disappointment go unrecognized. For example, someone may react with anger when they feel slighted, but behind that reaction, there could be an underlying fear of inadequacy or a need for validation. Developing emotional insight means learning to interpret anger as a messenger rather than an issue to be suppressed or ignored. This call for asking questions like:

- What am I protecting or guarding with this anger?
- What specific emotions or memories does this anger evoke?
- Are there parts of me that feel threatened, undervalued, or vulnerable?

These questions promote a mindset shift from viewing anger as a reaction to be avoided to one that indicates there is more to explore beneath the surface. This self-exploration helps people respond thoughtfully and recognize that their emotional reactions are windows into their own fears, anxieties, and unmet needs.

Getting to the bottom of fear and vulnerability

Fear is a common emotion that underlies anger, but it can be difficult to recognize at first. Often, anger becomes a way to hide or distract from feelings of fear or vulnerability that are more difficult to confront. For example, someone in a relationship may become angry when they feel distant or distant from their partner. Anger may appear on the surface as frustration, but the underlying issue could be fear of abandonment or rejection.

Developing emotional insight means recognizing these fears and accepting them as part of the human experience. Some introspective practices to uncover the fears behind your anger include:

- **Examine recurring anger themes:** Are there certain types of situations that trigger frightening anger? B. loss of control, degradation, or anxiety? Recognizing these themes can reveal underlying fears.

- **Practice self-compassion:** When fear arises, acknowledge it without judgment. Accepting fear as a natural part of life can reduce your tendency to react defensively.

- **Reflect on past experiences:** Do you have early experiences or formative memories associated with these fears? Understanding the source of your particular fear can reduce it and lessen its power over your current reactions.

Facing and accepting your fears can help you learn how to express them directly, rather than through anger. This openness can improve your relationships, as you will be better able to communicate your anxieties in a constructive way.

Identifying Anxiety as an Anger Trigger

Anxieties are also a big driver of anger. They are often related to self-esteem, competence, and social acceptance. When people feel anxious, they may lash out to protect their self-image or avoid feelings of inferiority. For example, someone may react angrily to criticism at work for fear that it suggests a lack of competence, or avoid social situations to avoid feelings of inferiority. Recognizing these anxieties can help you better understand how they affect your behavior and trigger your anger.

To explore your uncertainty, you can think about questions like:

- In what situations do you feel most anxious or inhibited?
- Do I have some fear about myself that I protect or hide through anger?
- How does my anger help me protect or distract from these insecurities?

Identifying these vulnerabilities allows people to work on self-acceptance, become less reactive, and be more willing to directly address the root of their insecurities. This approach allows them to build self-confidence and stronger self-esteem, thereby reducing the need for anger as a defense mechanism.

Consider Unmet Expectations and Needs

Unmet expectations and unmet needs are the main causes of anger and often stem from a discrepancy between what one wants and what reality offers. Whether it is for respect, affection, approval, or safety, frustration over these unmet expectations can lead to intense anger. For example, a person who feels that their hard work is constantly ignored may develop resentment and anger, reflecting a need for approval and validation. Understanding these unmet needs allows an individual to take proactive steps to meet them, rather than letting them fester and manifest as anger.

To develop emotional insight into unmet expectations, you need to:

- **Identify specific wants and needs:** What are my expectations in this situation that are not being met? Are these needs realistic and fair?

- Reassess your expectations: Are my expectations too high, rigid, or implicit? Anger can arise when implicit expectations are not met. Identifying and communicating these can help you reconcile reality with your personal needs.

- **Learn to express your needs directly:** Anger often arises when people expect others to understand their needs without communicating them. Developing the courage and ability to express your needs openly can greatly reduce frustration.

Understanding the role of unmet expectations can help you constructively direct your behavior toward meeting your needs, resulting in fewer disappointments that cause anger and greater emotional clarity.

Techniques for building emotional insight and self-reflection

Developing emotional insight is a gradual process that requires consistent reflection and self-exploration. Here are some practices readers can use to deepen their understanding of anger and its roots.

1. **Keep a journal:** Writing down moments of anger along with their associated thoughts, feelings, and possible triggers will reveal patterns over time. Journaling provides a safe space to explore deeper emotions and serves as a tool for tracking growth and self-discovery.

2. **Mindfulness meditation:** Practicing mindfulness helps people better recognize their thoughts and feelings as they arise. By observing anger without judgment, we can learn to recognize its presence early and explore its underlying causes without immediately reacting.

3. **Self-inquiry techniques:** Asking open-ended questions such as, "What do I really feel behind this anger?" or "What am I trying to protect or reveal with my anger?" can give understanding that changes indiscreet responses into amazing chances for development.

4. **Therapeutic guidance:** Working with a therapist, especially one trained in cognitive behavioral therapy (CBT) or psychodynamic therapy, can help individuals uncover the deeper fears and anxieties that trigger their anger. Therapy provides a structured space to safely explore these feelings and develop healthier coping strategies.

Turning emotional insight into positive change

Emotional insight is only valuable if it leads to actionable change. With a clearer understanding of what anger reveals about personal fears, anxieties, and unmet needs, individuals can begin to manage their anger differently. Rather than letting anger dictate our actions, we can use this awareness to make more conscious decisions, express our emotions honestly, and work on our personal growth.

Developing emotional insight ultimately transforms anger into a guide rather than an enemy. This enables people to understand their own inner landscape, recognize the vulnerabilities exposed by anger, and respond in ways that promote healing, resilience, and true self-expression. Developing this awareness lays the foundation for lasting emotional control, healthier relationships, and a balanced, fulfilling life.

Chapter 4:

Strategies for Immediate Anger Control

- ### *Breathing Techniques*:

Introduce calming breathing practices to regain control during an angry episode.

When anger flares up, it's as if the body automatically goes on high alert, resulting in a physical reaction that leads to words and actions we may regret. One of the most effective ways to interrupt this escalation and regain composure is through controlled breathing techniques. Proper breathing not only calms the body, but it also calms the mind, allowing us to pause for a moment, reflect, and choose a more conscious response. Here we explore a powerful breathing technique that can help you regain control when you're having a tantrum.

1. Deep diaphragmatic breathing: Harnessing the power of the diaphragm

Diaphragmatic breathing, also known as "belly breathing," can activate your body's relaxation response and counteract the fight-or-flight response that can be triggered by anger. This technique activates the diaphragm to encourage slower, deeper breathing, improving oxygen flow and signaling your brain to lower stress levels.

How to practice: Put a hand on your stomach and another on your chest. Breathe deeply through your nose, making sure your stomach expands to fill your lungs, not your chest. Breathe out slowly through your mouth, feeling your stomach collapse. Breathe in for four seconds, hold it for a moment, and then exhale for four seconds to try to prolong each breath. Repeat this multiple times until you feel more settled.

Why it works: Diaphragmatic breathing stimulates the vagus nerve and activates the body's parasympathetic nervous system (the "rest and digest system"). This slows heart rate, lowers blood pressure, and promotes calmness, all of which are important in moments of intense anger.

2. Box breathing (square breathing): creating a calming rhythm

Box breathing otherwise called "square breathing," is an organized procedure that achieves mental and actual concentration. This technique allows you to stabilize both the physical reactions of your body and the intense thoughts of your mind by following a set breathing pattern.

How to practice: Visualize a square. As you take in for four seconds, follow the main side of the square in your brain. Pause your breathing for four seconds while envisioning the following page. Exhale for four seconds on the third side of the square, then hold your breath for four seconds on the last side. Repeat the cycle, imagining the square being redrawn with each breath.

Why it works: This structured breathing rhythm grounds the mind in the present, creating a meditative effect. Box breathing slows your breath,

improves focus, and calms the physiological.
responses that accompany anger.

3. 4-7-8 Breathing: Slowing Down with a Long Exhale

From Dr. Andrew Weil, 4-7-8 breathing focuses on lengthening the exhale and bringing the body into a state of relaxation. This technique promotes a natural calming effect by emphasizing the exhale, and is especially useful for releasing intense emotions.

How to Practice: Begin by breathing in silently through your nose for a count of four. Hold your breath for seven counts... Then breathe out slowly and audibly through your mouth for a count of eight. Repeat this cycle for four rounds, or as many times as needed until you feel the transition to rest.

Why it works: Taking a short breath and then a long exhale activates the body's parasympathetic nervous system, lowering cortisol levels and slowing your heart rate. The long exhale also creates a feeling of relaxation, symbolically releasing any built-up tension or anger.

4. Alternate Nose Breathing: Balance Your Body and Mind

Alternate nostril breathing, known in yoga as Nadi Shodhana, is a technique in which you breathe through one nostril at a time. This exercise aims to balance the two hemispheres of the brain and harmonize emotional and logical responses.

How to Practice: Sit comfortably and close your right nostril with the thumb of your right hand. Breathe deeply through your left nostril and close your nose with the ring finger of your right hand. Breathe out through your right nostril. Then breathe in through your right nostril, close it, and exhale through the left nostril. Alternate this pattern, breathing slowly and evenly.

Why it works: This technique helps balance the energy between the brain hemispheres, calming the nervous system and promoting a balanced state of mind. Alternate nostril breathing is great for reducing anger by shifting your attention away from intense emotions and into a focused meditative practice.

5. Sigh Breathing: Release tension with targeted exhalation.

Sigh, breathing is a natural and easy way to release tension and quickly calm your nervous system. This technique is a simple way to emotionally reset by mimicking your body's natural response to stress - sighing.

How to practice: Breathe deeply through your nose, filling your lungs as much as possible. Then, breathe out through your mouth with a long, audible sigh, gently expelling all the air. Repeat this several times, focusing on the feeling of relaxation with each exhale.

Why it works: Sighing releases muscle tension in your body and activates your parasympathetic nervous system, which reduces the stress response associated with anger and helps you feel calmer instantly.

Make a habit of breathing exercises for effective anger management.

Practicing these breathing exercises regularly will help you deal with anger more constructively when it arises. Incorporating them into your daily life, whether during quiet times, your commute, or a busy day, will create a foundation for resilience and mindfulness. Over time, these techniques become automatic and reliable tools for stopping and responding thoughtfully when anger threatens to take over.

Breathing exercises are deceptively simple, but they have a powerful effect on de-escalating the body and mind. For men, especially, who have been raised to suppress their emotions, these techniques offer a way to acknowledge and deal with anger rather than suppress it, helping to foster healthier responses. Learning how to regulate your breathing can be the first step toward long-term anger control, leading to greater emotional balance and an overall sense of well-being.

• Mindful Distractions: Techniques to Prevent Impulsive Reactions

Explore the use of distraction techniques to prevent impulsive reactions.

When anger flares up, we often have the urge to react impulsively, whether with words, actions or, inner frustration. An effective way to manage such overwhelming moments is through conscious distraction. Unlike typical distractions that simply divert attention, conscious distraction allows you to intentionally focus on constructive activities or calming stimuli, allowing your mind to relax and gain clarity. This approach not only helps you avoid sudden reactions, it also promotes greater self-control and emotional resilience. Let's examine how conscious distractions work, why they are effective, and explore practical strategies for incorporating them.

The Science Behind Distraction as an Anger Management Tool

At its core, anger is an intense emotional and physiological response. When anger builds, the amygdala, the emotion center of the brain, overreacts, heightening the "fight or flight" state. This can impair your ability to think rationally, triggering an instinctual, often regrettable response instead. By consciously distracting, you redirect your energy away from the anger-provoking stimulus and toward a non-threatening activity, allowing your brain's prefrontal cortex (the area responsible for rational thinking and decision-making) to regain control.

Benefits of Conscious Distraction

Conscious distraction serves several purposes beyond simply distracting the immediate anger trigger. These techniques:

- **Provide a Mental Reset:** Focusing on another activity gives your mind space to process your emotions in the background, thereby reducing the intensity of your anger.

- Develop self-control: Regularly practicing conscious distraction practices helps you develop patience, control your emotional reactions, and pause before reacting.

- **Promote emotional balance:** By redirecting your energy into calming or constructive activities, you can release pent-up anger in a healthier way and reduce the overall impact on your mental and physical health.

Types of Conscious Distraction Techniques

There are a variety of techniques and activities that can help you consciously distract yourself. Here are some methods that are particularly effective when dealing with anger:

1. Sensory grounding practice

Sensory grounding is a technique that focuses on one or more senses to ground yourself in the present moment. By activating your senses, you can interrupt the flow of angry thoughts and clear a path back to calm.

- **The technique:** Try the "5-4-3-2-1" method. Distinguish five things you can see, four things you can contact, three things you can hear, two things you can smell, and one thing you can taste. This sensory inventory can help calm you and shift your focus away from what's making you angry.

Why it works: Activating your senses refocuses your mind from emotional turmoil to your physical environment, helping you ground yourself and reduce stress.

2. Physical Activity

Exercise is one of the most effective ways to channel intense emotions like anger. Physical activity diverts energy away from angry reactions while naturally releasing built-up tension.

- **The technique:** Take a brisk walk, do some jumping jacks, or do a calming yoga routine. These exercises can help redirect energy and lower the adrenaline and cortisol levels that rise with anger.

Why it works: Physical activity stimulates the release of endorphins, the body's natural mood-boosting substances, which can help counteract the negative effects of anger.

3. Artistic Expression

Creative activities offer a conscious and expressive way to deal with anger. Whether it's a sketch, a poem, or a short piece of writing, putting your energy into creating something can be a productive outlet for your emotions.

- **The technique:** Have a sketchpad, journal, or instrument handy. When you're angry, express those feelings through art, writing, or music.

Why it works: Artistic expression allows you to safely express and process your emotions. Creative expression taps into the brain's reward system, bringing feelings of peace and satisfaction, and allowing you to shift your attention from anger to a more positive sense of accomplishment.

4. Mindfulness and Meditation

Meditation and mindfulness practices are effective tools for grounding yourself in the present. Although they are often seen as calming techniques, they can also have a distracting effect by promoting focus and returning the mind to a neutral state.

- **The technique:** Try a short meditation session by focusing on your breath, imagining a peaceful place, or repeating a calming mantra. For a few minutes, set a timer, then unwind. Why it works: Meditation shifts your focus from the source of your anger to your breath, slowing your heart rate, lowering your blood pressure, and calming your mental state. Over time, meditation can also help you build resilience, making it easier to deal with situations that trigger anger.

5. Immerse yourself in nature.

Spending time outdoors or simply observing nature can be a grounding experience. Nature can provide a sense of perspective and calm, helping you release anger by focusing your mind on the calming, rhythmic patterns of the natural world.

- **The technique:** Spend a few minutes walking around your local park, sitting in your garden, or watching a nature video if you're indoors, such as the hues of the leaves, the sounds of the birds, and the sensation of the breeze.

Why it works: Studies show that spending time in nature reduces stress and improves mood. Observing the natural environment helps you feel calmer and reminds you that the intensity of your anger is temporary.

6. Solve a puzzle or engage in a cognitive distraction.

Engaging your mind in a cognitive activity such as solving a puzzle, playing a strategy game, or even sorting out small tasks can be an effective distraction from anger. This shift in focus activates your brain and helps you move from a reactive state to an active, solution-oriented state.

- **The technique:** Pick a crossword puzzle, Sudoku, or other mentally stimulating game. Or try organizing a small space that requires focus and precision, like a drawer or bookshelf.

Why it works: These activities help distract your mind by focusing on a constructive task. Engaging in problem-solving or cognitive tasks requires focus, leaving less mental space for anger.

Incorporate Conscious Distractions into Your Daily Life

Conscious distraction can not only help you in moments of anger but also as part of your daily habits to maintain emotional balance. When used proactively, these techniques can help you become more resilient and less likely to react when anger arises. Incorporating them into your daily routine, such as morning meditation, evening walks, and journaling, can provide a continuous outlet for your emotions and prepare you to deal more constructively with intense moments.

Over time, deliberate distraction can help you develop a more mindful approach to anger. Rather than letting anger dictate your reaction, these techniques can help you pause, redirect your energy, and choose a response that aligns with your long-term goals and happiness.

- ## Taking a Time-Out:

When anger arises, it often clouds our judgment and leads to impulsive reactions that we may later regret. A simple but highly effective strategy for dealing with intense anger is a "time-out". Just as a break can calm and refocus a child, a time-out can also be effective for adults, providing the space to regain control of their emotions. This technique advocates temporarily stepping back from the situation, providing the mental and emotional space needed to process anger more rationally. In this section, we will explain why time-outs are so important for anger management, their benefits, and how to implement them effectively.

The Science of Time-Outs: How Taking a Break Helps You Control Your Anger

When anger reaches its peak, the body triggers a "fight or flight" response, flooding the bloodstream with stress hormones such as adrenaline and cortisol. In this heightened state, the prefrontal cortex, the brain's rational center, is overshadowed by the amygdala, the emotional center. This "amygdala hijack" frequently results in violent, impulsive reactions. However, taking a break gives your brain and body a chance to calm down, allowing your prefrontal cortex to regain control and make clearer, more considered decisions.

A time-out interrupts immediate emotional reactions, making you less likely to act impulsively. It prevents anger from escalating and gives you a chance to think, breathe, and recalibrate before reconsidering the situation. By regularly practicing this technique, you can train yourself to create a pause between feeling and acting on your anger, thereby enhancing your resilience and emotional control.

Benefits of Taking a Break

When it comes to dealing with anger constructively, the simple act of stepping back for a moment can have huge benefits.

1. Regain Clarity: Taking a moment away from an anger-inducing environment allows for self-reflection and clarity, giving you time to understand why you're upset and if it's worth addressing.

2. Prevent Escalation: Rather than allowing the situation to escalate into an argument or conflict, time-out acts as a buffer, reducing the chance of damage being done.

3. Strengthen Self-Control: Practicing the discipline to withdraw builds self-control, a skill that can then be applied to other emotional challenges.

4. Reduce Stress Levels: Because a time-out calms the physiological response, it reduces the stress response in the body, thereby lowering blood pressure, heart rate, and anxiety levels.

5. **Promotes better communication:** Returning to a conversation after a cooling-off period allows you to communicate more thoughtfully and respectfully, strengthening relationships and building trust.

Implementing an effective time-out strategy

Taking a time-out is not just about walking away, but making a conscious decision to take a step back with the goal of regaining control. Here's how to set a time-out effectively and intentionally.

1. Recognizing the need for a break

Recognition is the first step. Take note if your emotions become stronger, especially if you feel physical signs such as a racing heart, clenched fists, or shallow breathing. Noticing these signs can help you determine when it's time to take a step back before anger escalates.

2. Communicate clearly

If you're arguing with someone, let them know that you're taking a short break to cool down instead of abruptly walking away. For example, saying "I will require a couple of moments to accumulate my thinking" "I will return shortly, so you can go on without concern, " and" You can keep away from mistaken assumptions and show that you regard the other individual's sentiments.

3. Set a time limit

Taking a break does not entail permanently avoiding the situation. Set a specific time, anywhere from 5 to 20 minutes, if necessary. This ensures that the break is a strategy to calm yourself down, not an escape from the situation.

4. Perform a calming activity.

Use your break to do an activity that helps you control your emotions. Try deep breathing exercises, a short walk, or stretching to relieve physical tension. These activities activate the parasympathetic nervous system, inhibiting the stress response and bringing calm.

5. Think about your emotions.

Once you have calmed down, think about what is making you angry. Are there deeper emotions at work, such as pain, fear, or frustration? Identifying these root causes can help you address the situation with a clearer understanding of your own emotional needs.

6. Come back with a new perspective.

After your time-out, approach the situation in a calmer, more constructive manner. Remember that the purpose of a time-out is not just to calm you down, but to help you deal with the situation more effectively. When you re-engage, you are more likely to be able to communicate productively and resolve the problem without letting running emotions get in the way.

Practical Tips for Taking Regular Breaks

Incorporating time-outs into your anger management toolkit takes practice and consistency. The following advice will help you develop the habit of taking breaks:

Schedule a time-out for stressful situations: If you know that certain situations trigger anger, schedule a time-out before emotions escalate.

Use visual or mental cues: When you feel tense, use a reminder, such as a specific phrase or mental image that tells you to take a break. For example, visualizing a red stop sign can prompt you to take a break.

Reward yourself for taking a break: Reinforce the habit by recognizing a positive outcome. Notice the difference when you return to a clearer mind.

Consider the outcome after the time-out: After the time-out, think about how it affected the situation. Positive outcomes reinforce the habit and motivate you to continue with it in the future.

Building a Habit of Stepping Away

Over time, time-out strengthens your emotional resilience and improves your anger management. It becomes an internal signal that helps you deal with the situation without being dominated by anger.

Consistently using a time-out not only improves your immediate reactions but also contributes to long-term emotional balance and mental clarity.

Final thoughts on the time-out technique

Time-out is a deceptively simple yet powerful tool to break the hold of anger over your mind and body. Temporarily stepping away from an emotionally charged situation creates space for rational thinking, returning clarity and perspective. It's a technique that anyone can use, and with regular practice, it becomes an invaluable part of a balanced approach to dealing with anger. Taking a step back doesn't mean avoiding or ignoring problems; rather, it allows you to approach them with a steady hand and a clear mind, promoting healthier relationships and a more peaceful inner state.

Chapter 5

Long-Term Strategies for Anger Management

• **Mindfulness and Meditation**

Explain how regular mindfulness practice can reduce reactivity and foster calm.

Mindfulness and meditation can provide significant long-term benefits in anger management by rewiring the brain's response to stressors and cultivating a more balanced and calm internal state. Regular practice of these techniques allows individuals to observe their thoughts, emotions, and triggers without immediately reacting, creating a buffer between angry feelings and impulsive behavior. In this section, we look at how mindfulness and meditation can help reduce anger, the science behind their effectiveness, and practical tips for incorporating them into daily life.

Understanding Mindfulness and Meditation in Anger Management

The practice of mindfulness involves giving your full attention to the here and now, without passing judgment. In the context of anger management, it is about observing the first signs of anger - thoughts, physical sensations, and emotional fluctuations - without automatically reacting to them.

Mindfulness means awareness and acceptance, allowing people to live with unpleasant emotions rather than reacting impulsively.

Meditation, often used to increase mindfulness, is a systematic practice in which people spend time focusing inward, usually on their breath, a mantra, or guided imagery. Meditation strengthens your ability to calm yourself when anger arises, and over time develops patience, emotional regulation, and self-compassion. When practiced consistently, mindfulness and meditation work synergistically to create a more balanced emotional landscape, making it easier to work through difficult situations without being dominated by anger.

The Science of Mindfulness and Meditation: Rewiring the Brain

Regular practice of mindfulness changes the brain in ways that directly affect how you deal with anger. Research has shown that mindfulness and meditation increase activity in the prefrontal cortex (responsible for rational thinking and controlling emotions) while decreasing activity in the amygdala (the brain's fear and anger center). These structural changes lead to greater self-control, empathy, and patience.

In addition, meditation lowers cortisol levels, which in turn lessens the stress response. This reduction in stress hormone levels can prevent a chronic anger cycle in which prolonged stress and tension reduce frustration tolerance. With less underlying stress, people are better able to deal with anger-provoking situations with a calmer, more measured response.

How Mindfulness and Meditation Reduce Reactivity

Mindfulness and meditation teach practitioners to observe their inner reactions with curiosity rather than judgment. Here's how they address anger specifically:

Slow down your immediate reaction: Mindfulness creates a pause between feeling anger and acting on it. This space is critical to allowing time to break reactive patterns and choose a response that aligns with your long-term happiness.

Increase emotion awareness: Paying attention to the emotions that fuel your anger helps you recognize when underlying emotions like pain, anxiety, or disappointment are triggering your anger. Understanding these underlying emotions often lessens anger and allows for a more thoughtful, less defensive response.

Builds empathy and compassion: Meditation, especially compassion-based practices, increases empathy and helps people view others with more patience and kindness. Anger is reduced in interpersonal conflicts because empathy allows for a more constructive and understanding approach.

Improves patience and resilience: Regular meditation practice promotes patience and emotional resilience. With a more resilient mindset, people are less likely to feel slighted or let frustration develop into anger.

Practical Steps to Build Your Mindfulness and Meditation Practice

Start Small with Focused Breathing: A basic mindfulness practice for newbies is to concentrate on your breathing. Sit quietly for 5-10 minutes a day and focus on your inhalation and exhalation. Bring your thoughts back to your breathing when they stray.. This focused breathing reduces anxiety, centers the mind, and reduces reactions when anger arises.

Recognize the actual indications of anger using a body check: Body scan meditation, in which you mentally "scan" each part of your body for tension, can help you recognize the physical signs of anger before they intensify. Noticing early signs, such as tightness in your chest or shoulders, can help you begin calming techniques before anger escalates.

Practice observing your thoughts without judgment: Observing your thoughts without judgment during meditation can help you break the cycle of negative self-talk that fuels anger. Acknowledge your thoughts as they arise, without dealing with or reacting to them. This detachment helps you reduce impulsive reactions in your daily life because it trains you to not identify so strongly with every angry thought.

Incorporate guided mindfulness sessions: Using guided meditation apps or videos can provide structure and support, especially for beginners. Sessions focused on controlling anger and cultivating compassion can be especially helpful in training patience and reducing reactivity.

Practice mindfulness daily: Beyond scheduled meditation sessions practice mindfulness in your everyday activities. Try to focus fully on everyday activities like eating, taking a walk, or cleaning. Engaging fully in these tasks can improve focus and promote a cool, calm mind, making you more resilient to anger triggers.

Long-term benefits of mindfulness and meditation in anger management

Consistently practicing mindfulness and meditation creates long-term changes and makes it easier to manage anger.

- **Improved emotional stability:** Mindfulness promotes emotional awareness and resilience, allowing you to deal with anger with stability and clarity.

- **Improved physical health:** Lower stress levels have positive effects on physical health, including lower blood pressure and improved immune function.

- **Improved self-compassion:** Meditation promotes self-compassion and reduces harsh self-criticism, which is often a hidden cause of anger.

- **Better relationships:** Practicing mindfulness in interpersonal situations increases patience, empathy, and understanding, promoting healthier, more compassionate relationships.

- **Improved happiness and life satisfaction:** By reducing the effects of anger and increasing positive emotions, mindfulness and meditation lead to increased life satisfaction.

Final Thoughts on Mindfulness and Meditation for Anger Management

Mindfulness and meditation are essential practices for anyone who wants to manage anger constructively. Though it may take time for the effects to appear, consistency will bring about lasting changes in how you process and respond to anger. By investing in mindfulness, people can not only reduce their immediate reactivity, but also cultivate inner peace that impacts all aspects of their lives, from relationships to mental health to overall well-being.

• Cognitive Restructuring

Introduce thought-challenging methods to reshape irrational beliefs that fuel anger.

Cognitive restructuring is a powerful psychological tool that helps change the way people think in anger-provoking situations. It involves identifying and challenging the irrational, unhelpful, or negative beliefs that often trigger angry reactions. This technique allows people to take a step back, critically evaluate their thoughts, and replace them with more balanced and constructive beliefs. This reduces the intensity of anger and encourages healthier responses.

Understanding the relationship between thoughts and anger

Anger is not just a reaction to external events. It often arises from internal thought processes, including interpretations, beliefs, and assumptions. For example, if someone gives you the right of way in traffic, the automatic thought that "they did that intentionally to disrespect me" can instantly lead to intense anger. However, when the thought is reframed to something more balanced, such as "Maybe they were in a hurry or didn't see me," the angry reaction subsides.

Cognitive restructuring teaches individuals to identify these "hot thoughts" or irrational beliefs and change them to alter their emotional responses. This is especially helpful for men, who tend to react aggressively, even aggressively, when they feel slighted, overlooked, or undervalued.

Recognize the irrational beliefs that fuel anger

Common irrational beliefs contribute to anger, such as:

- **Catastrophizing:** The belief that small mistakes or setbacks will become major catastrophes. For example, interpreting a small argument as a sign that the relationship is in serious trouble.

- **Mind reading:** knowing what others are thinking and assuming that their intentions are negative. For example, believing that a person's behavior is specifically intended to annoy or harm you.

- **Overgeneralization:** seeing a single event as a symptom of an ongoing, unchanging pattern. The thought that "I'm always being treated unfairly" can fuel anger and increase feelings of helplessness.

- **"Should" statements:** Making rigid demands on the behavior of others, such as "you should know better" or "people shouldn't treat me like that." When people inevitably fail to meet these high standards, anger results.

By identifying these unhelpful thought patterns, individuals can begin the work of restructuring their thinking patterns to lessen their anger. Cognitive restructuring does not mean ignoring or suppressing the anger, but rather developing a healthier, more rational perspective on the event.

Steps in Cognitive Restructuring for Anger Management

Cognitive restructuring involves a series of steps designed to help change the way an individual thinks about provoking a situation.

1. Identify the trigger situation and thought.

Start by identifying the situation that made you angry and the specific thought that accompanied that emotion. Writing down both the trigger and the thought can help you gain clarity. For example, if you feel angry when criticized, your thought might be, "Maybe you're criticizing me because you don't respect me."

2. Examine the evidence

Whenever you've recognized the thought, inspect and assess the proof for and against it. Ask yourself:

- Is there concrete evidence that my interpretation is correct?
- Is there an alternative explanation?
- Am I jumping to conclusions too quickly?

When we step back and examine the evidence, we often find that the thoughts that initially triggered our anger were exaggerated or based on assumptions rather than facts.

3. Challenge and Reshape the Though

Then challenge your irrational beliefs with more balanced thoughts. For example:

- **Original thought:** "You are intentionally disrespecting me."
- **Rearranged thought:** "Maybe they are managing their problems, or perhaps they don't know how their words impact me."

This approach reframes the situation, making it less personal and more objective. Switching from an emotional interpretation to a more rational one can help reduce your anger.

4. Practice self-compassion and patience

Anger often stems from the high expectations we have of ourselves and others. Practicing self-compassion -- reminding ourselves that mistakes are part of growing up and that everyone has bad days -- can help reduce anger toward ourselves and others. Allow for some mistakes rather than fueling anger with self-criticism or criticism, reducing the need for immediate defensive responses.

5. Replace absolutes with flexible thinking.

Replace "always" and "never" statements with more flexible language. Instead of thinking, "People always treat me badly," think, "Sometimes people are inconsiderate, but that doesn't mean they intentionally want to upset me." Flexible thinking reduces the intensity of anger by providing a more nuanced view of events. If possible.

Practical and thought-provoking techniques

1.The "what if" technique

Ask yourself "What if my beliefs are not accurate? "Creates room to consider optional explanations, often resulting in an even better interpretation of situations.

2.The double standard technique

Suppose you were advising a friend in the same circumstance. In many cases, we are more forgiving and compassionate toward others than we are toward ourselves. This technique can help you bring that same empathy within, reducing anger and seeing the situation more fairly.

3. Realignment

Reframing is the process of viewing a situation from a new perspective. For example: Instead of perceiving an attack, take criticism as a chance to grow or seek feedback. Reframing turns potential triggers into opportunities, reducing the likelihood of an angry response.

4. Cost-Benefit Analysis

How much does it cost and how much does it earn to keep this idea?" asks yourself. Even though anger is frequently accompanied by a sense of righteousness, balance the advantages (emotions in law) against the disadvantages (emotional distress, strained relationships, and health effects).

The Benefits of Cognitive Restructuring for Long-Term Anger Management

By consistently practicing cognitive restructuring, individuals can experience many benefits beyond anger management.

Improved Emotional Control: Reframing thoughts improves your ability to control your emotions, making it easier to respond calmly rather than reacting impulsively.

Improved Relationships: Cognitive restructuring reduces misunderstandings and defensiveness, allowing for more constructive communication and stronger connections.

Improved resilience: Restructuring helps individuals adopt a positive, adaptive mindset, making it easier to deal with difficult situations without resorting to anger.

Improved self-esteem: Transforming self-criticism into constructive self-reflection can reduce reflective anger and promote self-compassion, which leads to improved overall self-esteem.

Cognitive restructuring is the key to emotional freedom

Cognitive restructuring allows individuals to control anger by changing the way they interpret and respond to events. By challenging irrational beliefs and replacing them with a balanced, realistic perspective, a person reduces the impact anger has on them. This technique acts as a bridge between emotional and thoughtful responses, providing a sustainable path to emotional freedom and healthier, more fulfilling relationships.

• Building Resilience:

Guide readers in developing mental resilience to withstand potential triggers more calmly.

Resilience is the mental strength that allows you to overcome life's challenges with grace, especially in situations that may trigger anger. Increasing resilience does not mean suppressing emotions or simply enduring discomfort. Rather, it is about developing the ability to face difficult emotions such as anger, process them, and respond in a balanced way. Strengthening resilience enables people to deal with anger triggers more calmly, respond constructively to setbacks, and ultimately experience a greater sense of control over their emotional world.

Understanding resilience and its importance in dealing with anger

Resilience is the ability that helps you recover from adversity, stress, and mental distress. Resilience is crucial for people dealing with anger because it improves their ability to pause, reflect, and make conscious decisions in emotionally charged situations. A resilient mind assesses a situation from a balanced perspective instead of reacting impulsively, minimizing angry reactions and preserving mental and physical health. Resilience provides a buffer against anger by enabling individuals to deal with triggers without letting emotions dictate their behavior.

Key Elements of Resilience in Dealing with Anger

Increasing resilience involves strengthening certain skills and mindsets that allow you to calmly respond to life's provocations.

1. Recognizing Emotions: Resilience is based on understanding one's emotions, including anger, in real-time. The ability to recognize emotions as they arise allows for targeted responses rather than knee-jerk reactions. Self-awareness helps individuals recognize early signs of anger and manage them before they escalate.

2. Adaptability: Life's unpredictability often overwhelms us. Building adaptability, or the ability to remain flexible and open to change, helps us calmly handle unexpected challenges. Rather than clinging to specific expectations, adaptability allows us to respond to setbacks and triggers in a constructive manner, reducing our tendency to become frustrated or angry.

3. Mindful reflection: Regularly practicing mindfulness (observing thoughts and feelings without judgment) builds resilience by allowing individuals to gain a broader perspective on their emotions. Mindful reflection creates the necessary distance between us and potential triggers, allowing for a reflective rather than reactive response.

4. Positive self-talk: Resilient people have positive self-talk and counter negative inner dialogue with positive, rational thoughts. When triggers arise, resilient people are able to remember that they have the power to choose their response, reducing the feelings of helplessness that sometimes fuel anger.

5. Set healthy boundaries: Setting boundaries is essential to maintaining emotional health. Knowing when to back off or say "no" can help you avoid situations that may trigger anger, especially those that cross boundaries or cause unnecessary stress.

Practical strategies to develop resilience against anger triggers

1.Practice cognitive flexibility

Cognitive flexibility, or the ability to change perspectives, allows people to see a situation from different angles and minimize anger. For example, if a situation seems frustrating, cognitive flexibility encourages the affected person to consider alternative explanations. Instead of interpreting a colleague's curt tone as disrespect, you might think that the person is suffering from their own stress. This change of perspective helps to avoid unnecessary anger.

Regularly participate in stress-reducing activities.

Chronic stress is one of the most common precursors to anger. Resilient people actively participate in stress-reducing activities such as sports, yoga, and hobbies. For example, physical activity releases endorphins, improving mood and enhancing the brain's ability to deal with stressors calmly rather than aggressively. Regular stress reduction forms the basis of resilience, making it easier to calmly deal with anger triggers.

Strengthening self-regulation techniques

Self-regulation means controlling your own emotional reactions in the intense emotions of the moment. Techniques such as deep breathing, progressive muscle relaxation, and visualization can help you deal with sudden anger. Regular practice strengthens your resilience by helping you calm down even in stimulating situations.

Cultivating a Growth Mindset

Growth-minded people see challenges and setbacks as opportunities for personal growth. Rather than viewing triggers as personal attacks or injustices, a growth-minded approach encourages people to learn from each experience. This shift in perspective transforms potentially anger-inducing situations into opportunities for self-improvement, thereby reducing the likelihood of emotional outbursts.

Build a support network.

Resilience is often strengthened by strong social support. Being surrounded by empathetic, understanding people provides a buffer against stress and anger. Being able to talk to someone you trust allows you to vent your feelings constructively, which can reduce feelings of frustration and build emotional strength over time.

Build patience through gradual exposure.

Resilience is often the result of accumulated experience dealing with difficult situations. Practicing patience by gradually exposing yourself to small, manageable stressors builds the endurance needed to deal with larger ones without losing your temper. This exercise is similar to strength training. Just as a muscle gets stronger through gradual resistance, so does our emotional resilience when faced with small challenges.

Benefits of Resilience in Anger Management

Increasing resilience has many benefits for people dealing with anger, including:

- **Improved emotional control:** Resilience gives people the tools to control their emotional reactions, promoting a sense of calm and control in difficult situations.

- **Improved relationships:** By responding calmly and constructively to potential triggers, resilient people build healthier, more stable relationships. Some people also feel more comfortable in relationships with people who treat their emotions with dignity.

- **Reduced physical and mental stress:** Anger takes a toll on the body and mind, which can lead to stress-related illnesses. By building resilience, people experience less emotional stress, which also benefits their physical health.

- **Improved self-confidence:** Knowing you can handle difficult emotions boosts self-confidence, leading to a more confident mindset that is less susceptible to external provocations.

Building resilience as a lifelong process

Resilience is not something that happens overnight. It is an ongoing process of reflection, growth, and practice. By actively working on resilience, people can develop deep-rooted strengths that allow them to face life's challenges with clarity and calm. Over time, this resilience becomes an anchor that enables one to face potential anger triggers with the calm and composure necessary for a balanced and fulfilling life.

Resilience when dealing with anger is a journey, not a destination. Through regular practice and deliberate effort, individuals can build a stable foundation from which they can calmly address triggers, respond thoughtfully, and enjoy a greater sense of peace, regardless of external circumstances.

Chapter 6

Effective Communication and Conflict Resolution

• Expressing Anger Constructively

Teach readers how to express feelings without hostility or blame.

When handled poorly, anger can quickly cause conflict, undermine relationships, and destroy trust. However, when expressed constructively, anger can be a powerful tool for expressing emotions, addressing problems, and ultimately promoting healthier relationships. Expressing anger without hostility or blame is crucial to resolving conflicts in a productive and positive way. In this chapter, we explore techniques for expressing anger constructively to help people express emotions in ways that promote understanding, cooperation, and mutual respect.

The Importance of Expressing Anger Constructively

Being angry is a normal human emotion and is not always a negative thing. However, how you channel your anger can have a significant impact on the outcome of a situation. When anger is uncontrolled or poorly channeled, it often leads to arguments, misunderstandings, and even violence. Conversely, when anger is channeled calmly and thoughtfully, it provides an opportunity for problem-solving and emotional connection.

Expressing anger constructively requires a conscious, compassionate approach that focuses on solving the problem, rather than venting or blaming others. This approach fosters an open communication environment in which both parties feel heard, respected, and understood.

Key principles for expressing anger constructively

1. Put more emphasis on "I" statements than "you" statements.

One of the most effective ways to express anger constructively is to use "I" statements instead of "you" statements. Using "I" statements allows a person to express their feelings without blaming or becoming defensive. For example, instead of sounding accusatory like "You always ignore me," saying "I feel ignored when I'm not heard" changes the tone of the conversation and makes it more inviting, making it a more productive dialogue.

Why it works: "I" statements focus on the speaker's feelings and experiences, rather than the other person's behavior, reducing the chance of self-defense and encouraging a collaborative approach to problem-solving.

2. Acknowledge the emotion instead of attacking.

When we're angry, it's easy to fall into the trap of attacking or criticizing the person who provoked those feelings. However, this approach rarely solves the underlying problem and often escalates the conflict. Instead, it is important to acknowledge the feelings of anger and discuss the situation without resorting to blame.

For example, "I'm really frustrated because I feel like my opinion isn't being taken into account in this conversation." This statement acknowledges the anger while avoiding direct accusations, keeping the discussion more objective and non-adversarial.

3. Use calm, controlled language.

The words we use when expressing anger can either escalate or de-escalate the situation. Harsh words, insults, and yelling only increase anger, making it harder to find a solution. Instead, use calm, neutral language that clearly expresses your feelings without inflaming the situation.

For example, instead of saying, "I can't exactly talk to you! You can say, "I'm frustrated because I feel like no one will listen to me." This version expresses frustration but avoids hostile language that could lead to unfair behavior. Frustration can provoke defensive or combative reactions.

4. Describe the behavior, not the person.

Instead of attacking the person or their character, focus on describing the behavior or actions that caused the anger. This approach makes it easier for the other person to listen because it avoids generalizations and judgments that may feel personally attacked.

Example: "I was stressed out because the meeting took longer than expected because I had other things to do" instead of "You're always late and wasting time" The person is criticizing, which makes it hard to hear the real concern.

5. Stay focused on the solution.

Constructive expression of anger goes beyond just venting, it also leads to finding a solution. Once the anger has been communicated, the next step is to focus on how to resolve the issue in a way that satisfies both parties. Focus the conversation on finding constructive ways to move forward, rather than dwelling on the problem.

For instance: "It irritates me when decisions are made without consulting you. I would be happy if we could discuss any big changes together that are coming up. This statement doesn't just express anger, it suggests a positive, actionable solution."

6.Make sure your body language is respectful.

In order to identify anger, nonverbal communication is crucial. Crossed arms, clenched fists, or a tense posture can signal hostility, even if your words are calm. To express anger constructively, make sure your body language is open and non-threatening. Maintain eye contact, stay relaxed, and avoid gestures that may be interpreted as aggressive.

Why it matters: Non-verbal signals can either support or undermine your message. Aggressive or closed body language can intensify conflict, even if your words are calm.

Benefits of expressing anger constructively

1. Improved communication and understanding

Expressing anger constructively creates an environment where both parties can understand each other's feelings and perspectives. This openness fosters respect for one another and helps to dispel misconceptions. When we can express anger without hostility, we feel more heard and valued, improving the quality of our relationships overall.

2. Strengthening Relationships

When anger is expressed in a healthy way, it can strengthen relationships rather than weaken them. Expressing emotions thoughtfully and respectfully allows people to build deeper connections because it displays vulnerability and tolerance. This approach not only improves conflict resolution, but it also builds trust and intimacy over time.

3. Avoiding Escalating Conflict

Constructive expression of anger helps prevent conflict from escalating. When people use nonconfrontational language and focus on solutions, they are less likely to get into hostile arguments and ongoing tensions. Instead, they approach problems calmly and cooperatively, resulting in quicker and more effective solutions.

4. Less Resentment

Relationships can suffer when anger is suppressed because it can breed resentment. However, expressing anger constructively helps release pent-up frustration before it turns into bitterness. Expressing anger openly and respectfully can help clarify the situation and prevent small issues from escalating into larger, more harmful conflicts.

5. Better Emotion Control

Learning how to express anger constructively can help you better regulates your emotions. It promotes mindfulness, self-awareness, and emotional intelligence, which are key components of mental well-being. Over time, this habit can lead to improved emotional control, greater resilience, and more balanced responses to challenges.

• Assertive Communication Techniques

Introduce techniques like "I" statements to convey emotions without accusation.

Effective communication, especially in moments of anger or frustration, is essential to maintain healthy relationships and promote mutual understanding. One of the most effective ways to express emotions without assigning blame is assertive communication. Unlike passive or aggressive styles, assertive communication allows you to express your own emotions clearly and directly while respecting the other person's perspective.

The Power of "I" Statements

"I" statements are a fundamental tool for communicating confidently. They shift the focus from blaming others to expressing personal feelings and needs, preventing self-defense, and promoting open dialogue.

1. **Express emotions:** Start with how you feel about the situation. For example, saying "I feel..." as opposed to "You make me feel..."
2. **Describe the behavior or situation:** Describe objectively what occurred and keep away from accusatory language. "I get irritated when gatherings run long" rather than "You generally burn through my time".
3. **State a need or desired outcome.** Share what you want to achieve in the future and encourage a solution-focused approach. For instance: "I would see the value in it on the off chance that you could caution me ahead of time assuming if future meetings are going to be too long,

"I" statements allow the listener to comprehend the speaker's point of view without feeling attacked or held accountable. This is crucial to keeping the conversation constructive and reducing defensiveness.

Other techniques for assertive communication

Active listening: This technique makes both participants feel heard and appreciated. This includes listening carefully, nodding to show interest, and summarizing or reflecting on what has been said. Active listening can turn a conflictual conversation into a collaborative problem-solving session.

Use specific language: Avoid generalizations such as "always" or "never" that can escalate conflict. Instead, focus on specific events or actions. This will make the conversation more objective and less emotional.

Maintain a calm, neutral tone: Assertive communication relies on calm, even tone that signals control and respect. Try not to raise your voice and, if necessary, take a few deep breaths before speaking.

Set boundaries: Proactive communicators know their limits and are willing to set boundaries when necessary. This might include asking for a break to cool down during a heated argument or refusing a conversation that feels unproductive until both parties are ready to speak respectfully.

Avoid judgment and labels: Instead of labeling someone's behavior (e.g., "You're being unreasonable"), focus on how it affects you personally. This approach can lead to a more constructive response and prevent the conversation from drifting into blame and judgment.

• Conflict Resolution Skills:

Disagreements are inevitable in any relationship, but how you handle disagreements can either strengthen or weaken your relationships with others. Conflict resolution skills are designed to help you deal with disagreements in a way that maintains respect, stays calm, and promotes mutual understanding.

Key Conflict Resolution Techniques

Find common ground: Identify areas of agreement early in the conversation. This helps create a collaborative atmosphere and serves as the basis for finding a mutually beneficial solution. For example, if both people agree that they value honesty; this shared value can be the basis for resolving conflicts over trust and transparency.

Focus on the problem, not the person: When resolving conflict, it is important to focus on the specific issue and not attack the person's character.

This minimizes defensiveness and keeps the conversation on problem solving, not personal attacks.

Example: Instead of "You're always inconsiderate," say, "I felt overlooked when my opinion wasn't considered in the decision-making process." This phrase directly addresses the issue without attacking the person.

Work together to solve the problem: Instead of approaching conflict with a "win-lose" mentality, adopt a "win-win" mentality. When working together to solve a problem, both parties work together to find a solution that addresses the needs of both parties. This approach fosters collaboration and makes it easier to resolve disagreements without resentment.

Agree or disagree: Sometimes it can be difficult to find a middle ground. In these cases, it's important to respect each other's differences and accept that you may not be able to completely agree. Agreeing to disagree is a mature and respectful way to address disagreements without forcing compromises that are unsatisfying to either party.

Take responsibility for mistakes: When resolving conflicts, it's important to recognize your role in the disagreement. Taking ownership of mistakes not only shows humility but also encourages the other person to do the same, which can significantly reduce tension and increase mutual respect.

Timing and Setting: Address conflicts at a time and place where both parties can be calm and focused. Don't try to resolve issues in a stressful environment or when emotions are running high. A planned and calm setting allows for more effective communication and allows both parties to feel comfortable expressing their views without fear of interruption or escalation.

Benefits of Effective Conflict Resolution Skills

Developing strong conflict resolution skills has many personal and relationship benefits.

- **Improved Relationships:** Always resolving conflicts respectfully builds trust and mutual respect, strengthening relationships.

- **Improved Self-Esteem:** Dealing with disagreements calmly and respectfully increases self-confidence and reinforces a positive self-image.

- **Reduced Stress and Anxiety:** Unresolved conflict often leads to stress and anxiety. Constructive conflict resolution helps to reduce these feelings by addressing issues directly and calmly.

- **Improved Emotional Health:** The ability to communicate confidently and resolve conflicts effectively promotes overall emotional health and reduces the likelihood of resentment, anger, and frustration building up over time.

- **Improved Problem-Solving Skills:** Each time a conflict is resolved, your problem-solving skills are strengthened, making it easier to deal with future disagreements calmly and clearly.

Conclusion

By using assertive communication techniques such as "I" statements and mastering key conflict resolution skills, individuals can transform potentially destructive anger into constructive dialogue. These approaches emphasize self-respect, empathy, and clear communication, making it easier to resolve differences without causing lasting damage to relationships. Practicing assertive communication and effective conflict resolution not only reduces the frequency and intensity of conflict, but also builds a foundation of respect, understanding, and cooperation those enriches relationships and fosters lasting connections.

Chapter 7

Developing Emotional Intelligence

• Understanding Emotions Beyond Anger:

Educate readers on the full spectrum of emotions underlying anger, such as sadness, frustration, or fear.

Emotional intelligence is the foundation of effective anger management and emotional well-being. The capacity to identify, comprehend, and regulate one's own emotions as well as to sympathize with those of others is the foundation of emotional intelligence (EI).This skill is crucial when dealing with anger because beneath the surface there can be many intense feelings waiting to be understood. Anger is rarely a separate emotion; rather, it often masks more vulnerable feelings such as sadness, frustration, and fear. By exploring the full range of emotions underlying anger, readers can gain a deeper understanding of their inner landscape and develop healthier, more adaptive ways of dealing with life's challenges.

The Complexity of the Emotions Underlying Anger

Anger often acts as a shield against other emotions and arises in response to something painful, frightening, or frustrating. Examining these deeper emotions can help people gain insight into what is actually causing their anger and address the root cause rather than just the external reaction. Understanding these underlying emotions requires a willingness to be vulnerable and honestly examine the situation.

Some of the most common emotions underlying anger include:

Sadness: Sometimes anger acts as a defense against sadness, especially in situations involving loss, disappointment, or grief. For example, a person may express anger towards a loved one to avoid the sadness that comes with separation or hurt. Recognizing this connection can help affected people better understand the sadness behind their anger and address it head-on.

Frustration: Frustration is often a precursor to anger. It occurs when people feel they are unable to achieve their goals or meet their expectations, and they often feel helpless and impatient. Identifying frustration as a trigger can help shed light on why certain obstacles provoke such strong emotional reactions and allow you to manage your expectations or find an alternative solution.

Anxiety and Fear: Anger often masks fear and anxiety, as these emotions can make a person feel vulnerable or raw. For example, when a person fears failure, rejection, or loss of control, they may express anger to demonstrate their power or to regain a sense of security. By identifying the fear that underlies their anger, they can address their insecurity and learn how to deal with feelings of anxiety in a healthier way.

Shame and Guilt: Shame and guilt can also fuel anger, especially when a person feels judged or criticized by others or by themselves. Shame can lead to defensive anger, in which a person lashes out to avoid having to deal with feelings of inadequacy or failure. Recognizing that shame or guilt is triggers for anger can be transformative, as it allows for more compassionate self-reflection. Feeling disrespected or undervalued: Situations in which one feels one's values, opinions, or boundaries are disrespected can trigger anger. This reaction often indicates a deeper need for validation or recognition. Understanding this reaction can help people communicate these needs more proactively, rather than through anger.

Developing emotional awareness and vocabulary

A key part of emotional intelligence is developing an emotional vocabulary that helps identify and express these underlying feelings. Many people are accustomed to simply labeling emotions as "angry" or "happy" without exploring the more subtle nuances of the emotion. Increasing this vocabulary allows individuals to have a more nuanced understanding of their emotions and to respond more appropriately.

Consider common emotion descriptions such as frustration, disappointment, weakness, loneliness, and feeling hurt. Each word conveys a different aspect of the emotional experience. When people can accurately name and recognize these emotions, they are better able to deal with them appropriately.

An effective way to increase emotional awareness is to keep a diary of your daily emotional experiences and note situations that trigger particular emotions, such as anger. This reflection will help readers recognize patterns, gain insight into the root causes of anger, and learn more about the range of emotions.

Strategies for recognizing and dealing with underlying emotions

To increase emotional intelligence when dealing with anger, it is important to develop habits and strategies that allow for honest introspection and deeper self-awareness. Here are some approaches that may be particularly helpful:

Practice mindfulness: Mindfulness is about staying present and observing the emotions that arise without judgment. Practicing this habit can help people recognize underlying emotions that may lead to anger, such as frustration or sadness, before they escalate. By recognizing these emotions in the moment, we can learn to respond thoughtfully rather than impulsively.

Self-Reflection: Taking time each day or week to reflect on your emotional experiences can help you identify and understand what triggers your anger. Questions, for example, "What was I feeling before I got angry?" or "Was there another emotion behind my anger?" can provide valuable insight. Through introspection, a person can identify the root cause of their emotional reactions and develop deeper self-awareness.

Use cognitive techniques: Cognitive techniques such as questioning thoughts and cognitive restructuring can help reframe thoughts that may lead to anger. For example, if someone feels disrespected, they may realize that their feelings are based on assumptions or misunderstandings. Challenging irrational beliefs and cognitive distortions can prevent these emotions from escalating into anger.

Seek support and feedback: Discussing emotions with a trusted friend, family member, or therapist can provide valuable perspective. Often, others can offer insights or observations that the person may not have thought of. Having open conversations about emotions can reduce the stigma around expressing vulnerability and increase emotional intelligence.

Practice self-compassion: Cultivating self-compassion means treating yourself with kindness instead of criticizing yourself when you are emotionally conflicted. Recognizing that emotions such as anger, sadness, and frustration are part of the common human experience promotes acceptance, reduces defensiveness, and makes it easier to come to terms with the underlying feelings.

The Role of Emotional Intelligence in Anger Management

When a person goes beyond anger and develops a deeper understanding of their emotions, they are able to have more control over their reactions. Emotional intelligence allows a person to respond thoughtfully instead of reacting impulsively. They learn to recognize the early signs of escalating anger, acknowledge their true feelings, and respond constructively. This awareness and ability to manage emotions also improves communication skills, making it easier to resolve conflicts without resorting to anger.

Furthermore, developing emotional intelligence improves relationships, job satisfaction, and overall psychological well-being. People who are more aware of their own emotions tend to develop stronger connections with others because they are able to show compassion, actively listen, and respond with patience and understanding.

Conclusion

Anger is intense and often challenging, but when approached with emotional intelligence, it can be a guide to understanding deeper emotional needs. Recognizing that anger may have its roots in unexpressed feelings such as sadness, fear, or frustration opens the door to true self-discovery and growth. By exploring the different emotions that underlie anger, a person can not only manage their anger more effectively but also develop a deeper sense of self-awareness and resilience. In this way, they can develop a healthier, more balanced approach to their emotional world, and therefore live a more fulfilling and connected life.

• Empathy and Social Awareness:

Emphasize the importance of empathy in improving relationships and managing anger effectively.

Empathy and social awareness are key components of emotional intelligence, especially when it comes to managing anger and strengthening relationships. Empathy allows people to look beyond their own perspective to understand the feelings, thoughts, and needs of others, creating a foundation for mutual respect and connection. Closely related to empathy, social awareness involves recognizing and interpreting social signals such as body language, tone of voice, and context to assess how other people might feel or react. Both skills are invaluable for preventing misunderstandings, reducing anger, and building stronger relationships.

The Role of Empathy in Anger Management

Empathy plays a transformative role in dealing with anger. Anger arises when we feel misunderstood, wronged, or disrespected by others. Empathy allows a person to stop and consider the perspective and feelings of the other person involved beyond their own emotional response. Developing empathy can help us see a situation more objectively and reduce the intensity of our emotional reactions.

For example, in a conflict, an empathetic person may stop and consider the other person's motives and feelings rather than reacting defensively. Understanding that another person's behavior may be due to stress, anxiety, or their own challenges can help ease anger and shift the focus from blame to understanding. This change doesn't eliminate the need to set boundaries or express your feelings, but it does reduce intensity and allow for more respectful and constructive dialogue.

Empathy also prevents anger from turning into resentment. When people treat others with empathy, they are less likely to hold grudges and are more likely to discuss issues openly and kindly. This openness helps resolve conflicts early and prevents them from escalating or worsening.

Social Awareness: Sensing the Mood in the Room and Building Connections

Social awareness is closely related to empathy and allows individuals to understand their social environment and respond appropriately. This ability helps a person recognize cues that indicate how other people feel and what they need, allowing them to adapt their behavior depending on the situation.

In situations where anger may arise, social awareness can alert people to subtle signs that a conversation or interaction may be heading towards conflict. For example, if a person's tone becomes sharp or their body language becomes defensive, a person may respond patiently rather than annoyed. Recognizing these cues can help adjust one's approach by speaking more calmly or taking the time to actively listen, often easing tension and preventing misunderstandings.

In addition, social awareness contributes to emotion regulation by helping individuals stay grounded and aware of how their emotions affect others. When people are aware of their social environment, they become more thoughtful, attentive, and adaptive, improving the quality of their relationships and reducing the likelihood of anger.

Practice Empathy and Social Awareness

To develop empathy and social awareness, it helps to practice intentional, reflective actions that increase your ability to understand and connect with others.

Active listening: Listening to understand, not to react is the first step toward empathy. When interacting with others, focus on what they are saying without interrupting or planning retaliation.

Reflect on what you hear to confirm understanding and demonstrate consideration. This simple act shows respect, reduces misunderstandings, and often provides insight into the other person's emotional state.

Consider perspective: Get into the habit of considering the other person's perspective, especially in heated situations. Ask yourself, "How am I feeling now?" or "What might have caused me to behave this way? "Trying to control your reactions can be facilitated by this mental transformation.

Practicing Non-Judgment: Don't judge Approach conversations and interactions with a posture of curiosity rather than judgment. Rather than labeling a person's behavior as "wrong" or "irrational," try to understand what motivates their behavior. This change will reduce your emotional reaction and allow for a more productive interaction.

Observe body language and tone of voice: Develop a sense of nonverbal signals. Body language, facial expressions, and tone of voice communicate more than words and provide valuable insight into other people's emotions.

Being sensitive to these signals can help you adjust your responses to create harmony rather than conflict.

Verbally express empathy: When appropriate, let the other person know that you understand their perspective. It's tolerable to feel angry. "I can resolve this scenario because I am struggling at strongest."

• Emotional Regulation Skills

Provide exercises to help regulate emotions in challenging situations.

Emotion regulation is the ability to control intense emotions and prevent them from determining your behavior in a destructive direction. Mastering this skill is essential for anger management because it allows you to stay calm under stress, resist impulsive reactions, and respond to challenges constructively. Developing emotion regulation skills allows readers to face conflicts and frustrations with resilience and reduces the likelihood of being dominated by anger.

Here are some effective exercises to build emotion regulation skills:

1. Deep breathing exercises

Breathing techniques such as diaphragmatic breathing can help calm the nervous system, allowing you to regain control when anger begins to arise. Slow, deep breathing reduces your physiological response to stress by slowing your heart rate and calming your "fight or flight" response. Practicing deep breathing daily improves your body's natural relaxation response, making it easier to stay calm in hot situations.

Exercise: Try the 4-7-8 technique, which involves taking a 4-second breath, holding it for 7 seconds, and then slowly letting it out for 8 seconds. This technique will lower your heart rate and instantly relax you.

2. Mindful Observation

Mindful observation involves stopping to notice the feeling of anger without judgment or impulsive action. Rather than reacting, a person can observe their emotions as if observing from a distance. This practice creates a "buffer" that allows for thoughtful decisions.

Exercise: When anger arises, stop and mentally recognize your physical and emotional sensations. Are your fists clenched? Are you breathing shallowly? Accept these sensations without trying to change them, and take a few deep breaths. This basic perception assembles the distance between your feelings and your activities.

3. The Pause Technique

The "pause" technique is an effective way to prevent impulsive reactions. When an anger trigger arises, count to 10 in your mind before reacting. This delay gives you space to calmly consider the situation and reduces the risk of saying something unfortunate.

Practice: Practice counting to 10 whenever you feel something. Use this time to ask yourself if there is a different way to handle the situation and focus on responding constructively rather than reactively.

4. Cognitive reappraisal

Cognitive reappraisal is the process of reassessing a situation to see it from a less emotional perspective. When anger arises, this technique helps affected people to challenge irrational thoughts and replace them with a balanced perspective.

Exercise: In moments of irritation, ask yourself if your initial interpretation is correct. Is there an alternative explanation? For example, if someone gives way to you in traffic, consider that they may be in a hurry with an emergency rather than intentionally ignoring you. This change reduces the intensity of your emotions and prevents anger from escalating.

5. Self-Compassionate Statements

Practicing self-compassion reduces the shame and guilt that can increase anger. Practicing self-compassion allows you to acknowledge your problem without criticizing and be kind to yourself, thereby reducing your emotional response.

Exercise: During stressful moments, silently repeat self-compassionate statements such as B. "This is a difficult situation. It's tolerable to feel angry. "I can resolve this scenario because I am struggling at strongest."

Chapter 8

Transforming Anger into Positive Action

• Channeling Anger into Productivity

Guide readers on how to transform anger's energy into positive, goal-oriented actions.

Anger, with its intense bursts of energy and heightened focus, can be a powerful motivator when channeled positively. Although anger often has negative connotations, it is essentially an expression of dissatisfaction or frustration with the environment or something in one's life. Instead of leaving anger as a destructive behavior, people can learn to harness this powerful energy as a catalyst for positive change, personal growth, and productivity.

Understanding the Energy Behind Anger

Anger triggers a series of physiological responses that prepare the body for "fight or flight." This adrenaline rush, increased heart rate, and increased focus are part of the body's natural response to perceived threats and injustices. Instead of seeing anger as purely destructive, we can reinterpret it as an emotional warning that something important needs attention or change. Channeling anger requires catching its natural energy and utilizing it valuably. Anger often leads to impulsive behavior when left uncontrolled, but when it is contained and redirected, it can promote perseverance, innovation, and positive outcomes. Learning how to channel anger productively requires reframing it as a motivational force, understanding its roots, and channeling its intensity into beneficial activities and goals.

Strategies for Transforming Anger into Positive Action

Here are some techniques that can help you transform anger from a reactionary emotion into a productive, empowering force.

1. Set clear goals to direct your energy.

Outrage frequently comes from neglected assumptions or annoying issues. Use moments like these as opportunities to identify concrete goals that address the root causes of your frustration. Setting clear, achievable goals gives you an outlet for your anger and allows you to focus your energy on creating concrete, positive change.

- **Example**: If your anger is triggered by a career setback, redirect your energy by setting a professional goal to: B. learn a new skill or seek out a mentor for guidance. Channeling your frustration toward self-improvement transforms initially negative emotions into opportunities for growth.

2. Physical Activity as an Outlet

Physical exercise is a very effective way to release built-up tension and frustration. Not only does exercise calm the mind, but it also helps harness the physical energy generated by anger. Activities like running, weightlifting, and martial arts can help you release anger in a healthy way. Additionally, physical activity increases the production of endorphins, which combat stress, elevate mood, and promote a sense of calm and control.

- **Exercise habits:** By creating regular physical habits, especially ones you can rely on in moments of intense emotion, you can transform anger into strength and resilience, benefiting both your mental and physical health.

3. Transform anger into creative expression.

Creativity provides a meaningful outlet for intense emotions. Many artists, writers, and musicians use anger and other deep emotions as inspiration for their work. Whether through writing, painting, playing music, or even making crafts, creative activities allow anger to take new forms and give it a voice and a safe, constructive outlet.

- **Journaling:**

Writing in a journal about the source of your anger is an introspective practice that promotes clarity and self-awareness. This allows you to explore the emotions behind your anger, which can lead to insights and solutions.

- **Artistic pursuits:**

Engaging in creative projects, whether simple like a sketch or complex like a building project, can help you turn your anger into something positive, leaving a lasting legacy of growth and reflection.

4. Transforming anger into commitment and pro-social action

Anger at injustice, whether personal or social, can be channeled into commitment and meaningful change. Many social movements and reforms are driven by collective anger at injustice, and individuals can use that anger to contribute to causes and issues they care about. By channeling anger outward into constructive social action, individuals can have a lasting impact on the world around them.

- **Get involved:** Joining a community organization, participating in an awareness campaign, or volunteering for a cause that aligns with your values can give it meaning. This redirection of anger can help give it meaning, promote self-determination, and create a better environment for yourself and others.

5. Problem-Solving Approach to Address Triggers

When anger is triggered by a specific, identifiable problem, a solution-focused mindset can help redirect energy toward solving the underlying problem. Problem-solving helps break down what may seem difficult at first into manageable steps, providing structure and direction. It shifts the focus from venting anger to actively changing the situation, thereby transforming frustration into positive action.

- **Action Plan:** Create an action plan to address specific anger triggers. For example, if frustration at work is the source of your anger, establish steps to address that frustration, whether that be setting boundaries, learning a new skill, or seeking new opportunities.

6. Practice Mindfulness to Redirect Anger

Mindfulness practices, such as meditation and conscious breathing, can help individuals create a pause between their emotional response and their behavior. This pause allows people to intentionally redirect their anger instead of reacting impulsively. Mindfulness exercises help you observe your anger without judgment and choose a response that aligns with your personal values and goals.

Daily Practice: Incorporate mindfulness into your daily life to reduce your overall reaction to anger triggers. Over time, this habit helps build resilience, allowing people to channel their emotions productively even in stressful situations.

7. Transform Anger into a Self-Improvement Goal

Anger often provides feedback about areas in your life that need improvement. By reflecting on these signals, individuals can use anger as motivation to work on self-improvement such as B. becoming more patient, developing better communication skills, or learning emotion regulation techniques. Viewing anger as a source of information rather than a threat highlights areas of potential growth and sets the stage for personal transformation.

- **Self-Reflection:** Combining regular self-reflection with setting self-improvement goals can help anger bring about positive change and create an ongoing growth process that improves overall well-being.

Finding Purpose Through Anger

Encourage reflection on how anger can be a force for positive change when aligned with personal values.

Although anger is often viewed as a volatile and destructive emotion, when aligned with personal values and goals, it can be redefined as a powerful force for change. This redefinition of anger involves understanding its signals, uncovering its origins, and using it to drive constructive, meaningful, and life-goal-aligned action. For many people, anger is a response to feelings of injustice, unmet needs, and unmet desires, meaning it can be a deep motivator for positive change and fulfillment.

Reflecting on Anger and Finding Its Purpose

Recognizing anger as a messenger, not just a reaction, opens the door to self-discovery. When we pause to think about our anger, its causes, triggers, and the specific situations in which it occurs in our lives, we often find that it is intimately connected to our deepest values. For example, if someone frequently becomes angry when witnessing injustice, this may indicate a strong commitment to justice or compassion. By identifying these core values, individuals can use their anger as a guide to understand what is truly important to them and pursue aspirations that are consistent with these values.

1. Identifying the Core Values Behind Anger

Reflecting on anger can shed light on the values that are closest to us, often without us realizing it. By examining moments of intense anger, we can begin to see what beliefs or principles were challenged. This reflection can allow anger to act as a compass, guiding individuals to live their lives with more intention and integrity.

- **Reflection exercise:** Think back to a recent event when you were overwhelmed with anger. What was the central issue, and what personal values or beliefs were threatened or violated? Identifying these values can help you balance your anger with constructive actions that promote those beliefs.

2. Use anger as a motivator for positive change.

Anger doesn't have to be an isolated emotion. It can be a catalyst for constructive change. When you feel angry about a recurring problem, it's a signal that something needs to be done. Whether it's a personal situation or a larger societal issue, anger can motivate purposeful action that leads to growth and improvement. This could mean fighting back against injustice, improving personal relationships, or pushing yourself toward a meaningful goal.

- **Set targeted goals:** Use your anger as motivation to set clear, targeted goals. For example, if work-related stress often triggers your anger, this may be a sign that you need to pursue career goals that are more aligned with your personal passions and values in order to reduce work stress and feel more fulfilled.

• **Building a Life of Balance and Fulfillment:**

Explore the ways in which managing anger leads to healthier relationships, career satisfaction, and inner peace.

Anger left unchecked, can impair judgment, create relationship tensions, and even affect your physical health. But anger, when effectively controlled and redirected, can be a stepping stone to a balanced life filled with healthy relationships, career satisfaction, and inner peace. Achieving this balance requires targeted strategies for emotion control, self-awareness, and goal-directed action.

1. Build Healthy Relationships Through Controlled Emotion Management

If anger is not controlled, it can harm connections and protect truthful conversations.. Conversely, anger, when addressed constructively, can help build stronger, more honest relationships. Learning how to express anger in a healthy and confident way can promote trust and respect and build relationships based on mutual understanding and empathy.

- **Communication Techniques:** Developing confident communication skills, such as "I" statements and active listening, can help you express your emotions without blaming. This approach not only strengthens personal bonds but also encourages others to respond constructively, leading to more fulfilling interactions.

2. Achieving Career Satisfaction through Goal-Directed Decision-Making

Anger over professional issues, such as lack of recognition or ethical conflicts, often reflects a mismatch between work and personal values. Using anger as an opportunity to reconsider career decisions can help you make intentional changes that lead to increased job satisfaction and a sense of purpose. This may include pursuing a role that allows for greater creativity, freedom, or alignment with personal beliefs.

- **Career self-reflection:** Reflecting on work dissatisfaction can help you identify changes that will make work seem more meaningful. Whether it's taking on new responsibilities, looking for a new position, or pursuing a passion project, aligning your professional goals with your values will not only bring you a sense of satisfaction, but a fresh feeling of direction as well.

3. Cultivate Inner Peace Through Emotional Balance

Uncontrolled anger often creates a cycle of frustration and inner turmoil that undermines peaceful feelings. By learning to control and redirect anger, a person cultivates a calm, centered inner life. This calmness promotes resilience, enabling us to overcome challenges without being overwhelmed by reactive emotions.

- **Mindfulness exercises:** Regular mindfulness or meditation exercises can help maintain emotional balance. These exercises promote non-judgmental awareness of emotions and allow people to observe their anger, understand its causes, and decide how to respond calmly and thoughtfully.

4. Transform anger into compassionate action.

Anger that is rooted in empathy for others (such as indignation at injustice) can lead to compassionate, purposeful action. When anger motivates us to help others, it becomes a positive force that not only brings about external change but also deepens our connection with humanity. Acts of kindness, volunteering, or advocacy for a cause control anger in ways that benefit society and enrich personal fulfillment.

Volunteering and advocacy: When you participate in community and social engagement based on your values, you not only address the source of your frustration but also strengthen your sense of purpose and connection. Whether it is a small act of kindness or a large-scale effort at social change, such actions use anger constructively to bring about change.

Creating a balanced, fulfilling, and peaceful life

Controlling anger and finding meaning through it does not mean suppressing emotions; it is about understanding, accepting, and transforming them. When aligned with core values, anger can be a powerful guide to a balanced and fulfilling life. This change requires introspection, awareness of the emotion, and a willingness to transform anger into meaningful action.

Living a balanced life doesn't mean the absence of anger; it means the ability to respond to it clearly and purposefully. Through healthy relationships, adjusted career choices, and compassionate actions, people can not only live more fulfilling lives but also lives that are firmly rooted in personal values and inner peace.

Chapter 9

Practicing Forgiveness and Letting Go

• **Understanding the Role of Forgiveness:**

Explain how forgiveness—both of oneself and others—can reduce resentment and anger.

Forgiveness is often seen as one of the most difficult but rewarding practices for letting go of anger and resentment. It requires a deep, conscious decision to let go of the pain of past hurts and move forward with a lighter heart. True forgiveness is not about forgiving a harmful act or forgetting that it happened; rather, it is about releasing the emotional hold that a past insult has had on your mind and soul. In this section, we will explore the power of forgiveness not only as a way to improve relationships with others, but also as a transformational tool for self-healing and personal growth.

Understanding the role of forgiveness

Forgiveness plays an important role in managing and reducing anger. Without it, anger can become chronic, bubbling under the surface and manifesting as bitterness, resentment, and persistent stress. Forgiveness offers a path to inner peace by freeing people from the burden of clinging to past injustices. This act benefits not only the person who is forgiven but, more importantly, the person who forgives. Holding on to anger and resentment often creates physical and mental stress and affects overall well-being.

1. Let go of resentment and anger by forgiving others.

When someone wrongs us, it's natural to feel angry, hurt, and betrayed. But when we hold on to these feelings without finding a solution, we often hurt ourselves more than we hurt the other person. Forgiving others allows us to acknowledge the pain, but it also allows us to let go of the lingering effects of that pain. Through forgiveness, we release the emotional baggage of anger that can cloud our thinking and negatively affect our behavior.

Practice forgiveness: Look back on past grievances and examine how holding on to them affects your mood, behavior, and relationships. Then consider what it would feel like to let go of that resentment. This practice is not about trivializing injustice, but about putting an end to it within ourselves.

2. Self-forgiveness as a path to inner peace

Forgiving oneself is often the most difficult form of forgiveness, but it is essential for inner peace. Many people hold on to anger or guilt for past mistakes or perceived failures, which can hinder their ability to move forward. By recognizing that everyone makes mistakes and that self-compassion is essential for growth, we give ourselves permission to learn from our actions without being defined by them. Self-forgiveness allows us to let go of internalized anger, promoting an environment for personal healing and self-acceptance.

- **Self-reflection exercise:** Identify areas where you feel regret or guilt and write down the lessons you learned from the experience. Recognize these lessons as part of your personal growth and try to see mistakes as progress rather than shame.

The Healing Power of Forgiveness

Forgiveness has a profound impact on emotional and physical health. Letting go of resentment and anger has been proven to reduce stress, improve immune function, and increase optimism and happiness. Forgiveness isn't always easy or quick, but it's a worthwhile journey because it ultimately leads to a state of emotional freedom.

1. Forgiveness and Stress Reduction

Anger and resentment take a toll on the body, triggering a stress response that, if prolonged, can affect your physical health. Chronic anger has been linked to elevated blood pressure, heart problems, and increased susceptibility to disease. Forgiveness breaks the cycle of stress hormones and allows the body to return to a more balanced state.

- **Breathe and Let Go:** The conscious practice of deep breathing combined with visualizing letting go of anger can help promote a sense of calm. As you exhale, imagine the anger and tension leaving your body and being replaced by peace and acceptance.

2. Forgiveness and Improved Relationships

Holding on to anger distances us from others and creates barriers in our relationships. When we forgive, we become more open and compassionate toward others. This change not only improves personal relationships, but encourages a more proactive and empathetic approach to new connections.

- **Practice empathy:** When you forgive someone, try to put yourself in their shoes and consider their point of view, even if you don't agree with them. Understanding the other person's motivations and situation can make forgiveness easier and lead to greater empathy.

Letting Go: Leaving the Past

Forgiveness is only the beginning of the journey to emotional freedom. The next step is to let go of not only the anger associated with past grievances, but also the underlying desire to control outcomes. Letting go means freeing yourself from the shadows of past experiences and choosing to live in the present. It is a commitment to self-liberation that prioritizes peace and personal growth over resentment and resentment.

1.Embrace the present moment.

Choosing to let go allows you to fully engage in the present without being hindered by the pain of the past. This act of letting go frees up mental and emotional resources, allowing for more joy, creativity and openness in your daily life. It is an invitation to live consciously and focus on what really matters in the here and now.

- **Practice mindfulness:** Participate in mindfulness meditation regularly and focus on the present without judgment. When past frustrations arise, observe them without attachment and gently bring your attention back to the present.

2. Relinquish control and embrace transience

Letting go often means accepting that not everything can be changed, especially things that have already happened. It is realizing the transience of life and learning to appreciate each moment without getting stuck in old wounds. By letting go of the need for control, one can experience life with more freedom, less resistance, and more peace.

- **Practice acceptance:** Think about a situation that feels unresolved and consider the aspects you can control (such as your own reactions) and those you cannot (the actions of others). Accepting your limits of control will lead to greater peace of mind.

Embracing forgiveness as a lifelong habit

Forgiveness and letting go are not one-time acts but an ongoing process. It requires commitment, self-awareness, and a compassionate approach towards us and others. The practice is a form of self-care and self-empowerment, where people actively choose to release emotional burdens that no longer serve them. Through forgiveness, we gain peace, resilience, and openness to our life's journey, and are enriched by the freedom that comes with truly letting go.

Exercises for Releasing Grudges:

Offer practical exercises for letting go of long-held anger or grudges.

Holding on to a grudge may feel like it protects us from further harm, but in reality, it often traps us in a cycle of resentment, keeping our emotional wounds open and leaving little room for peace or progress. Conscious effort, empathy, and a readiness to let go of the past are necessary for letting go of a grudge. This section offers practical, introspective exercises to help readers let go of long-held anger and open themselves up to a life without resentment.

Exercise 1: Reflective Writing

Reflective writing is a powerful way to understand the roots of our anger. Writing can help us process emotions associated with past experiences and clarify the motivations behind our resentment.

- **Identify your resentment:** Start by making a list of the people or situations that provoke strong feelings of anger or bitterness. Write down the specific actions or events that triggered this resentment.

- **Explore your emotions:** Once you've identified your resentment, take the time to write about the associated feelings of anger, betrayal, sadness, disappointment, etc. Try to be as honest.

- **Challenge your assumptions:** Think about the assumptions you have about that person or event. What did you predict not being delivered? What examples could you at any point gain from this experience? By questioning your own beliefs and assumptions, you may find a path to empathy and understanding.

Exercise 2: Visualize Release

Visualization helps you emotionally and mentally prepares to let go. Creating an image of release in your mind helps you train your mind to move away from anger and embrace forgiveness.

- **Scenery:** Find a quiet place and close your eyes. Think about the person or circumstance you are angry with. Feel the emotions associated with this memory without judgment.

- **Imagine letting go**: Imagine you are holding a balloon that represents anger or resentment. Imagine releasing this balloon into the sky and letting it float away until it is out of sight.

- **Reinforce positive intention:** As you watch the anger fade, repeat phrases like: I am freed from their burden. This affirmation reinforces the act of letting go.

Exercise 3: Write a letter (Not Sent)

Even if you don't send the letter, writing a letter is therapeutic for expressing and processing your feelings toward someone who has wronged you. This exercise allows you to vent and express your emotions in a controlled, introspective way.

- **Write a letter:** Write a letter to the person who has wronged you. Honestly describe your feelings and how the other person's behavior affected you. Don't hold back. Acknowledge the full range of emotions, including anger, pain, and sadness.

- **Express a desire to let go:** In the final paragraph of your letter, state that you intend to forgive. This part of the exercise will help you let go and freely change your mindset from focusing on your complaints.

- **A physical symbol of letting go:** When you're ready, safely discard the letter. You can tear it up, burn it, or bury it to symbolically express your feelings.

Exercise 4: Practice empathy and perspective-taking

An effective way to let go of resentment is to practice empathy by looking at the situation from the perspective of the person who hurt you. This doesn't excuse their behavior, but it can help you gain a deeper understanding of their actions and motivations.

- **Understand the situation:** Consider the person's background, stresses, or conflicts that may have influenced their behavior. Ask yourself if their behavior reflects their own pain or limitations.

- **Seek humanity:** Remember that everyone makes mistakes. Practicing empathy humanizes the person and helps you see beyond their behavior, helping you recover from anger.

- **Transform resentment:** As you explore this perspective, consider how holding on to a grudge affects you and what freedom letting go can give you.

• Healing Emotional Wounds:

Discuss how releasing anger frees emotional space for growth, connection, and resilience.

When anger and resentment are released, the mental and emotional space previously occupied by resentment is freed. This openness allows for deeper healing and paves the way for growth, connection, and resilience.

1. Create Emotional Space for Growth

Letting go of resentment is like weeding a garden. By getting rid of what you no longer need, you allow healthier, more fulfilling emotions to emerge. Letting go of anger creates room for personal growth, building resilience, and learning from experiences that previously held you back. This newfound freedom allows you to invest your energy in self-improvement, relationships, or creative pursuits that align with your personal goals and values.

- **Personal Reflection:** Take time each day to reflect on what positive feelings and thoughts have surfaced since you let go of resentment. Noticing the positive effects of letting go can strengthen your commitment to this practice.

2. Build Stronger Connections

Resentment not only puts a strain on individuals, it often seeps into relationships, creating distance and tension. Letting go of resentment can help you build better relationships. This emotional release can lead to more meaningful, authentic connections, reaching out to others without the shadow of past slights influencing your interactions.

- **Reclaiming compassion:** As part of your journey to releasing anger, practice showing understanding toward others. This practice strengthens empathy, which creates healthier relationship dynamics.

3. Cultivate Emotional Resilience

To heal emotional wounds, you must develop the strength to face difficult emotions and turn them into learning experiences. When you let go of anger, you realize that while pain is inevitable, you can control your reactions. This resilience becomes a powerful tool not only for dealing with anger but also for dealing with future challenges with grace and calm.

- **Practice Mindfulness:** Strengthen your resilience by incorporating mindfulness into your daily life. Focus on observing your emotions non-attached so you can respond thoughtfully rather than reactively.

4. Find Inner Peace

Ultimately, letting go of long-held anger and resentment is the path to inner peace. When we let go of resentment, we give up the illusion that holding on to anger will change the past or protect us from future pain. Instead, we realize that peace is found in acceptance, compassion, and the decision to prioritize our own happiness over past grievances.

- **Daily Affirmation:** Start each day with an affirmation such as: "I choose peace over resentment" to shift your focus to inner harmony. Through these exercises and the work of releasing anger and healing emotional wounds, readers can take powerful steps toward a life that is balanced, open, and deeply peaceful.

Conclusion

A New Path Forward

At the end of this journey of understanding and controlling anger, it is time to reflect, plan, and commit to next steps. Once viewed as a purely destructive force, anger has been redefined as a highly complex emotion that, if thoughtfully managed, can promote deep personal growth, healthier relationships, and a balanced, purposeful life. This conclusion is intended to consolidate the journey so far and encourage readers to turn what they have learned into a personalized, actionable anger management plan and cultivate a mindset of ongoing growth and resilience.

• Reflection on the Journey of Anger Management

In our exploration of anger management, we have uncovered the roots of anger, analyzed its triggers, and explored the impact of anger on all aspects of life, from mental and physical health to relationships and careers. Anger is not inherently harmful. Rather, it is a natural human response that signals an unmet need, unresolved pain, or when a boundary has been crossed. The key is to recognize when anger is constructive and when it is a signal to stop and think.

Understanding the physiological, emotional, and behavioral aspects of anger helped readers recognize the signs of anger before it become overwhelming. By practicing techniques such as mindfulness, breathing, and cognitive restructuring, they developed tools to manage anger in the moment and promote emotional resilience in the long term. With these insights, anger was transformed from a destabilizing force into a tool for self-awareness and personal growth. The journey has not only been about controlling anger, but using it to uncover deeper layers of my values, fears, and desires.

• Creating a Personalized Anger Management Plan

Effective anger management is not a one-size-fits-all solution. It is a very personal journey and must be tailored to your individual needs, values, and triggers. Readers have learned about a range of strategies. The next step is to combine these tools to create a structured, personalized anger management plan. This plan will serve as a daily, actionable guide to help you stay grounded, prevent anger from getting out of control, and maintain emotional balance when faced with challenges.

1. Identify your personal triggers: Think about specific situations, environments, or people that often trigger feelings of anger. Identifying these triggers can help readers develop prevention strategies and proactive approaches to dealing with anger.

2. Choose an immediate technique: Choose the technique that seems most effective in that moment, such as breathing exercises, time-outs, or conscious distraction. Because everyone's body and mind respond differently, it's important to test and adjust these techniques until they feel natural.

3. Practice long-term strategies: Work to incorporate long-term strategies such as mindfulness, cognitive restructuring, and empathy training into your daily life. These practices will increase your emotional resilience and make anger management easier in the long run.

4. Set measurable goals: Your personalized anger management plan should include specific goals such as reducing the frequency of tantrums, improving communication in difficult situations, and building deeper, healthier relationships. Setting measurable goals helps readers track their progress and stay motivated.

5. Build a support system: Find friends, family, or a support group who can encourage you and hold you accountable. Connecting with others who understand your goals can strengthen your commitment to change and provide guidance during difficult times.

Developing a personal anger management plan is an important step forward. This book helps readers address anger in a way that respects their personal experience and provides the resources they need to overcome life's obstacles with calm and purpose.

• Commitment to Ongoing Growth

Anger management is not a destination, but a lifelong journey. Like any personal growth effort, controlling anger requires ongoing effort, regular self-reflection, and a willingness to learn from each experience. Readers are encouraged not to view anger management as a one-time solution, but to embrace it as an evolving practice -- an ongoing commitment to self-awareness, emotional balance, and self-control.

1. See setbacks as learning opportunities: Moments of anger are not failures. They are opportunities to learn more about you. By reflecting on each tantrum, readers can identify patterns, pinpoint areas for improvement, and modify their anger management plan accordingly.

2. Celebrate progress, no matter how small: Acknowledge and celebrate every step toward healthier anger management, even if it's a small success. This positive reinforcement will boost your confidence, motivation, and pride on the road to emotional balance.

3.   Practice forgiveness: Forgiveness, both towards oneself and towards others, is a key part of anger management. Letting go of guilt and resentment allows readers to create mental and emotional space for growth and move forward with confidence.

4.   Strive for self-care: Effective anger management goes hand in hand with self-care. Prioritize your physical health, mental well-being, and emotional needs as fundamental components of maintaining a balanced and resilient mindset. Self-care is not a luxury, but a necessity to effectively manage your emotions.

5. Review and revise your plan: As life progresses, your sources of stress and frustration change. Regularly review and update your anger management plan to reflect your current needs, values, and goals. This will ensure that your approach to anger management is appropriate and effective, and can adapt as needed to new stages and challenges in life. Final Thoughts

Embarking on the anger management journey is a transformative decision that opens the door to deeper self-awareness, richer relationships, and a more powerful ability to deal with life's inevitable challenges. By choosing to understand, redirect, and constructively manage anger, readers can not only improve their own lives, but also positively impact those around them.

The anger management journey is both challenging and rewarding. With patience, commitment, and an open heart, readers can harness the energy of anger for personal empowerment and build a life that is balanced, fulfilling, and peaceful. Embarking on this journey means living true to yourself, staying true to your personal values, and approaching each day with the strength to turn challenges into opportunities for growth. Ultimately, controlling anger is more than just controlling emotions; it's about living a life of purpose, emotional intelligence, and deep personal resilience. Each moment of self-mastery brings readers closer to a life filled with meaning, peace, and the freedom that comes from mastering self-control, not just anger.

THE END

www.ingramcontent.com/pod-product-compliance
Lightning Source LLC
Chambersburg PA
CBHW061338250726
48657CB00004B/1222